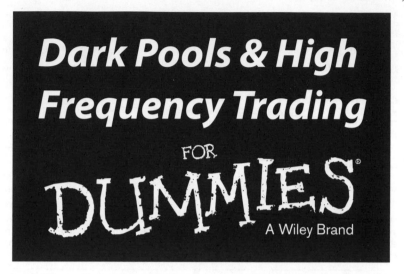

Dark Pools & High Frequency Trading

FOR DUMMIES®

A Wiley Brand

by Jay Vaananen

Dark Pools & High Frequency Trading For Dummies®

Published by: **John Wiley & Sons, Ltd.,** The Atrium, Southern Gate, Chichester, www.wiley.com

This edition first published 2015

© 2015 John Wiley & Sons, Ltd, Chichester, West Sussex.

Registered office

John Wiley & Sons Ltd, The Atrium, Southern Gate, Chichester, West Sussex, PO19 8SQ, United Kingdom

For details of our global editorial offices, for customer services and for information about how to apply for permission to reuse the copyright material in this book please see our website at www.wiley.com.

Wiley publishes in a variety of print and electronic formats and by print-on-demand. Some material included with standard print versions of this book may not be included in e-books or in print-on-demand. If this book refers to media such as a CD or DVD that is not included in the version you purchased, you may download this material at http://booksupport.wiley.com. For more information about Wiley products, visit www.wiley.com.

Designations used by companies to distinguish their products are often claimed as trademarks. All brand names and product names used in this book are trade names, service marks, trademarks or registered trademarks of their respective owners. The publisher is not associated with any product or vendor mentioned in this book.

For general information on our other products and services, please contact our Customer Care Department within the U.S. at 877-762-2974, outside the U.S. at (001) 317-572-3993, or fax 317-572-4002. For technical support, please visit www.wiley.com/techsupport.

For technical support, please visit www.wiley.com/techsupport.

A catalogue record for this book is available from the British Library.

ISBN 978-1-118-87919-1 (hardback/paperback) ISBN 978-1-118-87929-0 (ebk)

ISBN 978-1-118-87930-6 (ebk)

Printed in Great Britain by TJ International, Padstow, Cornwall

10 9 8 7 6 5 4 3 2 1

Contents at a Glance

Table of Contents

Introduction

Really only a few completely understand the domain of dark pools and high frequency trading (HFT). Even experienced finance professionals have a limited understanding of how both work. In fact, many still remain baffled. However, because dark pools and HFT have gone mainstream, more and more professionals and investors are interested in discovering as much as they can. Now you can't read the business pages without someone discussing dark pools or HFT.

The discussion around dark pools and HFT is the most divisive in finance at the moment. Despite the fact that the operators of dark pools and the traders behind HFT algorithms are slowly being forced out into the open to discuss their actions, much remains a mystery.

From flash crashes to theories about rigged markets and billions in profits made out of tiny changes in prices, dark pools and HFT are a part of modern markets. If you aren't knowledgeable in how they work and affect your trading, you'll be bait for the sharks.

I've spent my career as a private banker, dealing with and managing large amounts of money, finding myself and my clients up against high frequency traders, and using dark pools to get the best possible price for my clients.

Dark Pools and High Frequency Trading For Dummies shows you the ins and outs of dark pools, including what dark pools are, how they differ from a traditional stock market and how HFT has made day trading next to impossible. I have written this book for the savvy investor who has experience with stock markets and knows how stocks are traded on an exchange. This book is also helpful if you're a finance professional, particularly if you're in a client-facing role.

About This Book

If you're an active investor or a financial advisor, you're already more than likely aware of the growth of HFT and the use of dark pools. You've watched the prices on an exchange and seen some strange movements. With or without your knowledge, trades you have been involved with have most likely been conducted in a dark pool or executed against a high frequency trader, or even both.

The difficulty that you may have had is the lack of information as to what your role is and what your effect is in these circumstances. Some literature out recently has discussed dark pools and HFT, and the pages of newspapers are also full of information. The problem is that most information you read leaves you either feeling that it fails to explain what is really happening or that it's too technical and difficult to understand. This book corrects that.

Whether you're an experienced financial advisor or an active investor, this book gives you a clear overview of how the modern market works and what you can do to avoid yourself, or your clients, becoming victims of predatory algorithms. This is all set up in the easy to understand Dummies format.

Within this book, you may note that some web addresses break across two lines of text. If you're reading this book in print and want to visit one of these web pages, simply key in the web address exactly as it's noted in the text, pretending that the line break doesn't exist. If you're reading this as an e-book, you've got it easy – just click the web address to be taken directly to the web page.

Foolish Assumptions

I made the following assumptions about you when I wrote this book. I assume that

- You already have experience in investing or managing your and/or other people's money.
- You've heard about dark pools and HFT and already have an interest in the subject.
- When you've bought or sold stocks, you suspect that the trades may have been executed in a dark pool.
- You're willing to accept that there are unfair practices in the financial markets.
- You're trying to find ways to invest and trade better while operating against high frequency traders.
- You would like to know how different dark pools work.
- You understand that trading in markets is risky.
- You aren't naive enough to believe what financial services providers tell you.

No matter whether one or all of these assumptions applies to you, I'm confident that you can find tons of useful information to help be better informed as you wade through dark pools.

Icons Used in This Book

The icons that appear in the book's margins can help you navigate your way through the book. Here's what they mean.

This icon calls out suggestions that help you to work more effectively and save time when investing in dark pools.

You'll see this icon when I want you to pay special attention to an important piece of information. You can keep those pieces in the back of your mind for regular reference.

These icons point out moments that can cause potential risk or problems. Pay special attention to them.

Beyond the Book

You may find every now and then that you need some additional information or just a quick recap about HFT and dark pools.

In addition to the material in the print or e-book you're reading right now, this book also comes with some access-anywhere goodies on the Internet. Regardless of how good your memory is, you can't possibly remember everything related to dark pools and high frequency trading, so check out the free Cheat Sheet at www.dummies.com/cheatsheet/darkpools, which will bring back the most important points about dark pools and high frequency trading.

You can also find more helpful tidbits of information and advice online at www.dummies.com/extras/darkpools, including being aware of the risks of dark pools, the basics of automated trading and ten things you need to know about dark pools.

Where to Go from Here

Like every other *For Dummies* book, this book isn't linear, so feel free to start anywhere you like, jump around and read about what you want that interests you. Peruse at your leisure. Because I've assumed that you're already a savvy investor, you may read some information that you already know inside out. Go ahead and skip it and just read the stuff you don't know. Start by having a look through the table of contents to find what catches your fancy.

Keep this book close by whenever you're investing and planning on entering an order into the market. If you're a finance professional, you'll get questions about dark pools from clients. Having this book as a reference nearby helps you sound like the professional that you are.

Part I
Getting Started with Dark Pools

You can discover more about what dark pools and high frequency trading (HFT) are, some basic fundamentals of HFT and other helpful pieces of information about dark pools at www.dummies.com/cheatsheet/darkpools.

In this part . . .

✔ Explore the world of dark pools and find out why darkness is necessary to so many market participants and how it isn't necessarily a bad thing.

✔ Discover the differences between dark pools and traditional stock exchanges and how dark pools became so popular.

✔ Check out how the modern securities markets work after the arrival of dark pools and high frequency traders.

✔ Understand how a typical dark pool transaction is conducted from order to execution to confirmation.

Chapter 1

Focusing on Dark Pools and High Frequency Trading, Just the Basics

In This Chapter

▶ Looking at what makes a dark pool

▶ Defining high frequency trading

▶ Naming the cast of characters

▶ Identifying the order types

▶ Eyeing regulation

*T*hey're the hot topic in financial markets now. You can't open a newspaper or click on financial news without coming up against the terms *dark pools* or *high frequency trading (HFT)*. It's all happening in the world of dark pools – lawsuits, scandals and accusations of the market being rigged. One thing is certain: all the banks and brokers are involved in one way or another with dark pools. But whenever you mention dark pools, you also have to consider the subject of HFT. One came about because of the other, and then they came full circle and now both operate in the same environments.

Like the name implies, dark pools are dark and secretive and the banks, brokers and institutions that operate the dark pools would prefer them to remain that way. High frequency traders are no different; they're even more secretive about their activities and would've liked nothing more than to have stayed hidden in the shadows, buying and selling stocks in milliseconds and making money.

The world has changed, though, and now there's no hiding in the dark anymore. The light is being shone on dark pools and HFT. This chapter serves as your jumping-off point into that world.

HFT, dark pools and algorithms can be found anywhere where there's a working stock exchange. There's no place to hide from them if you want to invest in the markets. The United States remains the main market by far. With more than ten stock exchanges and dozens of dark pools, the venues are so fragmented that the US market remains the best type of market for high frequency traders to operate in. When it comes to changes and trends in the high frequency and dark pool market, look to the United States first – the rest of the world is sure to follow.

Defining Dark Pools: Why They're an Investment Option

Dark pools have been around in one form or another since organised stock exchanges began. In their simplest form they're a venue other than the stock exchange where stocks are traded. A *stock market* is one big, ongoing auction with investors and traders bidding and offering shares at different prices. Stock markets display their orders in an order book for all to see. When investors agree on a price, a trade happens and the process of agreeing on a price and making a trade repeats itself and continues all through the trading day as long as the stock exchange is open. But other times an investor may want to do a trade outside of an exchange.

That's where a dark pool comes in. A *dark pool* is a private venue where investors can exchange large amounts of stock without tipping the market to their intentions and, most importantly, without overly moving the market price. The common attributes of a dark pool are as follows. You can also refer to Chapter 2 for more detailed information about dark pools.

- ✔ **Little transparency of trade execution:** The broker, bank or whatever entity that is running a dark pool has a huge responsibility of discretion towards its clients to keep the information private and to make sure that information about a large order doesn't leak. Trying to find buyers without letting anyone know there are sellers and vice versa is challenging.

- ✔ **Trades executed within the spread:** The *spread* is the price difference on a stock exchange between a *bid* (a price someone is willing to buy a stock at) and an *offer* (a price someone is willing to sell at). A dark pool will benchmark the price it trades at to the prices on a stock exchange with the aim of doing the trade at a slightly better price for both the buyer and the seller. By settling a trade within the spread the price will be better than the price for both buyer and seller on the displayed stock market because the buyer receives a lower price than on the stock exchange and the seller gets a higher price than he would get on the stock exchange. Dark pools tend to be cheaper than a stock exchange because they don't have the same fees.

✔ **Owned by a bank or broker:** Banks and brokers are keen to use dark pools because it saves them from having to pay the exchange's fees. Although stock exchange fees seem small, just fractions of a cent, for a bank or broker they add up. It's much more cost effective to be able to match a trade internally in a dark pool.

Thanks to superfast computers and the ability to route trades through many locations inside of a millisecond, for many banks and brokers dark pools have become the first point to try to execute a trade before routing it to a stock exchange.

There are now dozens of dark pools all over the world. Brokers often first try to settle a trade between their own clients (called *internalising*) in their own dark pool. If they can't find a match, they will then route it to another dark pool, trying to find a match. Often the last port of call will be the traditional stock exchange.

On the darker side of the dark pool market, trading outside the displayed markets may give the broker an opportunity to take a small extra slice. Accusations have been made and even fines levied against some dark pools due to actions that haven't been in the clients' favour. Because of little transparency in the market, trading venue providers may be tempted to try to skim the little extra bit for themselves. *Trading venue providers* are those who operate a dark pool, most often banks and brokers. (Refer to Part IV for some risks associated with dark pools.) As a result of the suspect behaviour of some dark pools, legislators have stepped in to regulate and protect the investor. Head to the later section, 'Regulating the Markets: Legislators Take Action', for more information.

The growth in dark pools in recent years has been accelerated by the growth in HFT.

The evolution of dark pools and HFT

The modern dark pool market was created and has grown as large as it has because of high frequency traders. As HFT became better at detecting big orders, large institutions felt they were being used as fodder for the high frequency traders. They then wanted to hide from the high frequency traders and execute their trades out of sight of the algorithms. This is why dark pools were so attractive to big investors.

Now the situation has come full circle. The dark pools became successful businesses and therefore they wanted to grow. This meant they needed new traders in their pools and some opened the doors to high frequency traders and let them into the dark pools to trade. Now there are dark pools that allow high frequency traders in, the very group they were invented to keep out.

Explaining What High Frequency Trading Is

High frequency trading (HFT) is the use of algorithms to trade shares at a high velocity of turnover, sending orders to the market in large numbers and using computer algorithms at great speed. Thousands of trades are sent out and executed inside milliseconds, and it all happens at a pace faster than the human eye can detect.

Here are the defining parts of HFT:

- **Run by fast algorithms:** An HFT algorithm tries to catch tiny differences in the price of a stock – just a penny or even a fraction of a penny. It tries to repeat that thousands and thousands of times a day, so those pennies add up quickly into big money. Chapter 7 takes a closer look at algorithms.

- **Fast computers are co-located with exchanges:** High frequency traders are able to do what they do by using fast computer algorithms and placing their own computers close to the stock exchanges' own computers. Refer to Chapter 10 for more information on co-location.

- **Use of special order types:** *Special orders* are complex buy/sell orders used by algorithmic trading programs that define how an order is placed in a market, how it's shown on the order book and how it interacts with changes in the order book. Head to the later section 'Eyeing the special order types' for more.

- **The sending out and cancellation of lots of small lot orders:** High frequency traders send out small orders of 100 to 200 shares at a time, trying to find information about larger, hidden orders. They then trade against those orders to make a profit. Chapter 10 provides more information.

For a while HFT was touted as bringing down the cost of investing and trading in the markets, but as information about the nature of HFT started to leak out, cracks began to appear. Some players in the markets started criticising HFT as something that gave an unfair advantage to some, using predatory behaviour and taking advantage of other investors.

This debate split financial professionals into two camps. Some defended HFT as bringing down trading costs and providing liquidity, making the market a better, well-oiled machine. Then there were those who argued that HFT was akin to the market being rigged and should be outlawed. What's clear is that some shenanigans have been going on, and often the retail investor and the large institutions have been on the receiving end of the antics of some high frequency traders.

My experience with dark pools and HFT

I first got interested in dark pools and HFT when, as a private banker, I started noticing funny (not funny ha-ha; I mean funny as in strange) things happening when placing trades on the markets for my clients. The price would suddenly move against me, only to immediately move back to the original price after my execution was done at a less favourable price. Then there were the times when I placed an order in the market and it wouldn't appear on the order book. I'd call my trader, asking what was wrong. He'd call the broker (yep, we still used phones in the early days) who would confirm that the order was in the market, but still I couldn't see it. Round and round we'd go. Like a Christmas pantomime. My trader and broker telling me, 'Oh yes it is!' about my assertion that the order wasn't in the market, and me saying, 'Oh no it isn't!'

This situation started to get on my nerves, so I started looking into what was going on, asking questions and doing research. This led me to dark pools and HFT. At the time I had no idea how all-encompassing these two things had become for the market. The amazing thing was that so few top market participants, fund managers and CIOs had any idea of what was going on.

Through my research and the reach of my website, www.bankersumbrella.com, I've got to interact and discuss HFT and dark pools with many influential people on both sides of the HFT debate. I've learned a lot and continue to follow closely the changes in the market. I try to report on these matters and explain them in an easy-to-understand format, both on my website and on Twitter.

Knowing Who's Involved When Investing in Dark Pools

All those involved in the financial markets are in some way involved with dark pools and HFT. Some swim deeper in the pools than others, and some investors actually having no idea that their trades are involved in the world of HFT and dark pools. To grasp how the world of dark pools works you need to know who's involved, to what extent and how their activities might affect you. Chapter 5 looks at the cast of characters involved in dark pools and what their responsibilities are.

Brokers can make or break you

Brokers are the ones who match the trades. They find buyers for sellers and sellers for buyers. Without brokers there would be no market. In the world of dark pools and HFT, brokers operate their own dark pools and also run their own algorithms that execute trades and route orders to exchanges and dark pools.

The actions of brokers have a direct impact on you getting the best or worst out of your trade, so it's important for you to know how brokers operate, particularly how your own broker operates.

The other important folk

Plenty of other important operators are involved in dark pools. Here are the main ones. Turn to Chapter 5 for information on what role they play in dark pools and HFT.

- ✔ **Banks:** Banks operate their own dark pools in which they match trades for investors. Originally, banks' dark pools matched trades from their own clients, but their dark pools have grown to include high frequency traders and outside investors.

- ✔ **High frequency traders:** High frequency traders make up a large amount of the daily trading volume today, both in the displayed markets and now also in dark pools. They send out large amounts of small orders, trying to make a profit from tiny changes in the prices of stocks.

- ✔ **Large, institutional investors:** Investment fund managers and pension funds use dark pools and their own trading algorithms to try to disguise their large orders so their orders have as small a price impact on the market as possible.

- ✔ **Regulators:** Regulators monitor and enforce the laws regarding trading and markets.

Looking at the Order Types

To buy or sell stock in the markets, you need to send out an order that defines what it is you want to do with a stock (buy/sell), at what price and how many shares. Buy or sell orders used to be a rather simple affair, but in recent years order types have become more numerous and complex as HFT has evolved. Originally, only a handful of regular order types made trading in markets possible.

With the emergence of dark pools, multiple trading venues and algorithmic trading, special order types have been created that add a whole new level of complexity to trading. Knowing about both the regular and the special order types is important so that you can know which to use and how you can get the best of your trades. These sections give you a quick overview.

Considering the regular order types

The regular order types come in a few basic forms. Some orders execute immediately at the current price and others execute at a limit price. All orders include the amount of shares to be bought, sometimes with an additional caveat of only showing a certain amount of the order. Head to Chapter 8 for the ins and outs of these regular order types.

Eyeing the special order types

Special order types are complex and have many different criteria in addition to the regular order types. Literally hundreds of these special order types exist, with each market venue having its own. The one thing they all have in common is that they have been designed for use by algorithmic trading programs. Chapter 9 examines the most commonly used special orders in dark pools and explains what you need to know if they're right for you.

Regulating the Markets: Legislators Take Action

Legislators have taken an interest in HFT and dark pools because it's their job to set the rules that provide a fair market to all investors. HFT was born out of legislation, or perhaps a more apt description is to say that it was born out of legal loopholes.

As technological changes have outpaced legislative changes, new, superfast trading algorithms and computers have made it possible to execute trades faster than the eye can see. The speeds have become so fast that regulators haven't had the tools or expertise to see what's really going on in the markets. Regulators are now catching up with HFT and trying to crack down on those operators whom they suspect of trying to manipulate the market and take advantage of other investors.

Now legislators from all over the world are trying to block those loopholes. Doing so is a difficult task, but one thing is sure: more lawsuits and more legislation are sure to come that will change how both dark pools handle, route and execute their orders.

Legislation will also affect high frequency traders, and as a result the HFT market will also change, with some players unable to adjust to the new ways of doing business and new players taking their place. Refer to Chapter 6 for an in-depth discussion on how legislators are trying to regulate dark pools and HFT.

Information is a winner-takes-all race

HFT has become so fast that when news breaks that has an effect on market prices the price movement is over within a millisecond. There's no way you can compete in this market without the same speed as the high frequency traders and the best algorithms. The speed has become so fast that it is in fact a winner-takes-all race, with the first one to make the trade on the news being the one who takes all the profits. Refer to Chapter 10 to see how the information game is important in HFT.

Chapter 2

Taking a Dip into Dark Pools

*T*he term *dark pools* has been bandied around in the past few years in the financial world. What are they? What happens in them? Who runs them? The name is actually far more sinister than the real thing. *Dark pools* are simply places where stocks are traded 'off exchange'. In other words, they're an alternative to stock exchanges.

Stocks were traditionally traded in a stock exchange. Now, thanks to computer algorithms and increased volumes in stock trading, these new venues called dark pools have sprung up where stocks are traded. They pool together different investors' orders and match them up. In fact, they do exactly what an exchange does; the only difference is that executed trades aren't disclosed to the public immediately.

This chapter examines dark pools and explains what they are, how they operate and why they came about. This chapter tells you how they evolved and changed as the market changed and how they operate today. I also explain the pros and cons of dark pools and what you need to know to determine whether they're right for you.

Taking a Snapshot of Dark Pools: What They Are and Aren't

Dark pools have many similarities with a traditional stock exchange. Both are venues where stocks are bought and sold by traders and investors. There are, however, significant differences in how orders are priced and matched with each other in a dark pool and in a stock market. These sections show you exactly what dark pools are and what they aren't, so you can decide whether and when they are a good place for you to execute your trades.

Settled outside the public eye

Trades that are settled (also often referred to as *executed*) in a dark pool aren't immediately reported publicly. Usually, they're reported to the exchange sometime after the trades have been done. The timeframe of reporting trades differs from venue to venue and can also be dependent on the local financial rules and regulations. When the trades are reported after the fact and not in real time, there is less likelihood of a significant price impact on the stock.

Need for secrecy: Dark versus lit

Dark pool trades are anonymous and they aren't immediately reported, which is why they're referred to as *dark*. Any market that isn't a stock exchange quoting its trade data in real time is a form of dark pool.

On the flip side, traditional stock exchanges rely on transparency and openness. To exchanges, the very idea of a fair market is that all trading data regarding price and volume is open, which is why stock exchanges are referred to as *lit* markets. Today's global market place is a combination of trading done in the dark or in the lit markets.

You may think that the anonymity and secrecy of dark pools sounds sinister. However, allowing trading and the settlement of trades to be done out of the public eye, and in real time, is important for a couple of reasons.

Getting orders matched without moving the market

Brokers and banks have some options at their disposal to match orders without moving the market, which means that the price of the stock doesn't move while the order is being filled. Supply and demand affect market prices. Big sell orders increase the supply and can push prices down. Large buy orders increase demand and can therefore push up prices. Before the emergence of dark pools, a large institution could make a large order in only two ways:

✔ **Try to settle it between brokers after trading hours.** There are set hours when a stock exchange is open for trading. By agreeing to a price and amount of shares when the stock market is closed for trading, a large order will not move the market price.

> ✒ **Put the order into the displayed market.** If the whole order with it's full volume is displayed, the price will likely move against the institution because its order is so big that it moves the price of the stock. To counteract this, the smart option is to break the order into several parts, drip-feeding it into the markets by sending in orders in smaller 100 or 200 share lots. When these orders are filled the process would be repeated. This process can be laborious, and in fact advanced standard order types (see Chapter 8 for advanced standard order types) were planned to address this issue by automatically slicing a big order into smaller parts.

Algorithmic computer trading was created to sniff out these types of orders and then trade against them. Institutions were then faced with a need to find an alternate solution to their larger orders being adversely affected by the algorithms.

Making more profit by avoiding exchange fees

Brokers and banks could make more profit because their trades wouldn't be subject to exchange fees. The business of a stock exchange is to match trades. Each time a trade is executed, a stock exchange charges a fee, which is how stock exchanges make their money. Brokers liked the idea of dark pools because they could bypass the stock exchange and not pay any exchange fees and so increase their own profits. All the brokers needed to do was find buyers and sellers among their own clients and match those trades.

Improving price

Brokers have a duty to their clients of *best execution*, which is trying to find the best possible price for their clients. Part of the concept of best execution is *price improvement*, which means the opportunity, but not the guarantee, of getting a better price for their clients. If a broker has the opportunity of getting her client a better price in a dark pool as opposed to a displayed stock exchange, she can then route the client's orders to a dark pool.

Because prices in a dark pool take their prices from the bid and offer of the displayed exchange it and are often executed at the *midpoint* (average price) of the best bid and offer available on the displayed markets this gives the opportunity for a better price. Because prices can move very quickly, the opportunity for price improvement can be lost while the trade is being routed and the client ends up with an inferior price.

The *midpoint* of a trade is the average price between the best bid and the best offer; this way both the buyer and seller are satisfied because they get a slightly better price. For example, if a stock's best bid is $10.50 and the best offer is $11.00 and you'd like to sell your shares immediately, you'd receive the best bid of $10.50. If another buyer at the same time wanted to buy immediately, she'd have to pay $11.00. A dark pool would match these orders together at the midprice, which is $10.75. This way you, the seller, get $0.25 per share more for the stock and the buyer pays $0.25 less for her stock. Both of you get a better price than you'd have got in the stock exchange. This is a dark pool working at its best, delivering value to both sides of the market.

Examining How Dark Pools Work: Step by Step

Dark pools have become an important part of the global markets, and they're used as a viable alternative to stock markets. Knowing how they work will help you in your investing and help you to decide whether you want your trades to be routed through a dark pool and, if so, which one. This section discusses the ins and outs of how a dark pool works, from sending an order to executing an order.

In the days before dark pools, when you entered a trade your broker would place it in the appropriate exchange and that would be that. If you placed a *limit order*, an order that stipulates an exact price at which you're willing to trade a stock, it would be displayed in the order book. If you were watching the trading book in real time and the stock was one that was trading slowly enough, you could actually spot your order coming into the book. The number of shares and the price you instructed would pop up on the exchange's book. Here is what happens when you invest in dark pools:

1. **If your bank or broker has their own dark pool or has access to other dark pools, they may place your order there first before routing it to an exchange.**

   If you're using a limit order and the stock you're trading is one that moves slowly and isn't very liquid, a telltale sign of orders being routed via a dark pool is if your order doesn't show up on the order book.

   With an *at-market* order, which is an order that says you will make a trade at the best price on offer at that moment, your trade should be executed at the mid-price of the bid or offer if your broker is using a dark pool. (Refer to Chapter 8 for additional information about limit orders and at-market orders.)

2. **If the order is routed through a dark pool and there is an *opposite matching order* in the pool (a buy order to match your sell order or a sell order to match your buy order), your order will be executed there.**

At worse the price you get should be equal to the bid or offer available on the displayed stock market. Ideally, though, the price you get will be the midpoint of the bid and offer available in the displayed stock market. (Check out the earlier section 'Improving price' for more about the midpoint.)

3. **If there is no matching order in the dark pool, your broker may then route it to another dark pool and try to match the trade.**

   If a match still can't be found then the order is routed to the stock market. If it's an at-market order then it's executed immediately. If it's a limit order, it's placed on the order book until the price of the stock matches the price in the limit order.

4. **If the order is matched in a dark pool, it will then be reported to the exchange.**

   This doesn't happen in real time. Different countries have different rules as to the timeframe in which a dark pool transaction must be reported.

Weighing the Rewards and the Risks

Trading through a dark pool has both risks and rewards. One thing dark pools have done is brought more complexity and more choice to the markets. Here you can find out about the risks and rewards involved in a dark pool transaction and how to prepare your trading strategy for the potential risks.

Identifying potential rewards

Trading in dark pools has two main rewards:

✔ **Less price impact:** If you're trading in large orders or you're trading in shares that are *illiquid* (not traded actively in the market) then any order you send into the displayed market has the risk of moving the price in the direction that you don't want it to move. For example, when you send a sell order, you obviously want as high a price as possible for the stocks that you're trying to sell. Sending in a large sell order when not as many buyers are visible in the stock market will move the price down.

Also, when the order is displayed it sends a signal to the market that there is a large seller and buyers will pull their orders out of the market, anticipating that they will soon be able to buy the stock at an even lower price. This pushes the price of the stock you're selling down further.

But when it comes to sending the order to a dark pool, the size of the order isn't displayed, so your order has less likelihood of moving the price adversely against you. So one of the rewards of dark pools is to be able to buy or sell stock without moving the price against you.

✔ **Better price than the displayed markets:** The standard way to match a trade in a dark pool is to do it in the *mid-price of the spread*, which means that the price at which a dark pool trade is settled is the halfway point between the *best bid* (the highest price someone is willing to buy the stock at) and the *best offer* (the lowest price someone is willing to sell at).

If you want to buy a stock immediately, you pay the best offer. If you want to sell, you receive the best bid. The bid is always lower than the offer. By trading within the midpoint of the spread, the seller will get a slightly higher price than the best bid, and a buyer will get a slightly lower price than the best offer. When you're trading large orders in stock, or if you're trading often, this ability offered by dark pools to match trades at the mid-price can save you a significant amount of money in the long run.

Recognising the risks and preparing for them

Trading in dark pools has two main risks. They basically come down to the following:

✔ **Information leakage:** *Information leakage* is when other traders are able to receive information about orders coming into the market and use that information to profit from their own trading. When a large order is sent to a dark pool, no volume is shown, but it does and can leak information. For example, if a buy order is sent into a dark pool and it comes back unfilled or only partially filled, that shows that there aren't as many sellers in the market as there are buyers. This information has a tendency to leak and affect the price. Just as in a traditional exchange, when there are more buyers than sellers the price moves up. Whenever investors make an attempt to buy or sell, they're sending a signal to the market regardless of whether it's made in the dark or in the lit markets. Refer to Chapter 12 for more information about information leakage.

If you're a retail investor investing in small share lots then you don't need to worry about information leakage, because your trading won't have a great effect on the price of the shares.

✔ **Trust:** Any investor who uses a dark pool places a great amount of trust in whoever is operating the pool. When you place an order into a dark pool, the operator of the pool will have knowledge of the order. With that knowledge, the operator could trade ahead of the client (known as *front running*; refer to Chapter 12 for more information), or the operator could sell the information to a third party who could then do the same. Both of these issues are widely discussed when it comes to dark pools.

If you're concerned about trust, consider whether you trust your broker not to use predatory high frequency traders for liquidity. If your broker does, you could well find yourself often getting a worse price than what you expected. If you don't trust your broker then you may need to find another broker. Refer to the later section 'Asking your broker the right questions' to make sure that your broker is providing you with the best service.

To develop trust with your broker, your broker needs to be open with you about how she routes your trades and what specific dark pools she uses. Your broker needs to show that she follows and is up to date on the debate and public discussion on dark pools and HFT. Doing so shows you that she is competent and is able to adapt to any possible changes in how dark pools work and are regulated.

Investigating Whether Your Trades Are Exchanged in Dark Pools

Brokers aren't often upfront with their clients about how they route their clients' trades. Sometimes you may notice that you enter an order into the market and it doesn't show up on the exchange's order book. This can be particularly apparent in a slow-moving and illiquid stock; it's likely that your broker is trying to execute the trade in a dark pool.

Your broker may execute in a dark pool without asking you. Nothing is wrong with doing so if it helps you get a better price for your transaction. But dark pools do have some risks (which I discuss in the previous section), so you want to know if and when your trades are being executed in a dark pool and whether doing so is to your advantage or your broker's advantage. These sections explain what to do to ensure that you get the best from your trades.

Asking your broker the right questions

In order to find out whether your trades are being executed in dark pools, the best thing to do is to discuss the matter with your broker. Remember that dark pools can be good for you because they give you the opportunity to get your trades matched inside the spread of the displayed market and therefore get a better price. There is nothing inherently sinister about your broker using a dark pool, so the more you know about how your order is routed, the more it increases the chances of you getting a good price for your trade.

To have that discussion with your broker (or bank), come right out and ask whether your broker uses dark pools and which dark pools she uses. Seek to have a phone or face-to-face conversation so that you can have an open dialogue. Be sure to follow up on that dialogue with a written letter or email outlining your discussion; you want to keep some form of proof about the matters you have addressed with your broker about dark pools. Here are some additional questions that you can ask to uncover important information:

- ✔ **Do you have a default action regarding when orders are routed to a dark pool and when directly to an exchange? Or is it just at your discretion?** This question can tell you what route your order is likely to take and what venues it will go through. If any dark pools have been fined or are under investigation then you'll know which dark pools to avoid.

- ✔ **Do you accept payment for order flow? If so, from whom?** Some brokers accept payment from third parties, often high frequency traders, so that the brokers send their orders first to the entity that is paying for the order flow. *Order flow* can contain important, market impacting information and those whose orders are part of that order flow are at risk of predatory traders. In the United States, brokers are obligated to inform if they accept payment for order flow, but remember to ask, because it's always in the fine print.

- ✔ **Where have my executed orders been routed during the past six months?** In the United States, a broker is obligated to supply this information to her clients. This information will show you if your broker has a preference for certain markets. If so, be sure to ask why.

Check out the Cheat Sheet at www.dummies.com/cheatsheet/darkpools for more questions to ask your broker.

Sleuthing on your own if you don't use a broker

After you know what dark pools your broker uses, look them up. Chapter 4 includes some of the main providers. Investigate the providers online and look for any specific knowledge of how they match trades. You can also check Google News for any recent news related to the dark pools in question. Things change quickly in the finance world, so you can verify whether there are any problems or issues related to said dark pools.

Making the Best of Your Transactions

Dark pools aren't necessarily bad. They can help you get a better price for your stock transaction, provided your trades are regularly executed within the spread. Going through a dark pool is a positive thing if you're trading in an illiquid stock. Also, if you're trading a large volume of stocks then trading it through the lit markets might have a significant impact and move the price of the stock against you.

Although HFT can be toxic to your trades, not all HFT is predatory. If you're not consistently seeing your trades slip and are getting them executed at or within the spread then there's no need for concern.

Make sure your broker is upfront with you about what dark pools she uses and how she routes her orders. Doing this gives you the best possible information on how you can swim safely in a dark pool. If problems come to light, such as lawsuit or regulatory fines, you can always ask your broker not to route through a particular venue.

The good news for you is that you have options – you can instruct and ask your broker to route the order in a certain way or to a certain venue. If she doesn't do this, there are plenty of other service providers to whom you can move your business. Changing brokerage accounts is a simple process nowadays. Start by asking in writing if the broker can serve you in the way that you want. Also research to see whether there is any public discussion related to the broker's use of dark pools. If you're satisfied with both outcomes then you can safely transfer your business.

After the decision to invest, what happens during the order routing process is the second most important part of your trade. If you don't feel confident in your brokerage provider and you don't have adequate information as to how she executes your orders, then you need to change providers.

Chapter 3

Grappling with the Ins and Outs of Securities Markets

. . . .

In This Chapter

▶ Getting the lowdown on pricing

▶ Understanding the importance of liquidity

▶ Routing an order

. . . .

K nowing how a securities market functions is important to understanding how dark pools work. In fact, dark pools function much in the same way as traditional stock exchanges, including bid and offer, liquidity and market makers. If you have a basic knowledge of traditional stock exchanges then you should have little trouble grasping how dark pools generally work. This chapter takes a closer look at the similarities between traditional securities market functions and dark pools.

Figuring Out Pricing: The World of Bids and Offers

Dark pools and the stock market are similar when it comes to pricing. Each one is a giant *auction house* where investors and traders try to buy or sell at the best possible price. As long as the exchange is open, trading can be done constantly.

As an investor, you need to understand how and why prices move and how the system is set up. Even though the markets have become more complex, certain principles remain the foundation of all financial markets. Knowing these principles helps you to understand how a price is formed, how it moves and, more importantly, why it moves.

Dark pools take their pricing from the displayed stock exchanges. The daily trading of a stock on a displayed exchange involves four price points:

- ✔ The opening price
- ✔ The closing price
- ✔ The highest price
- ✔ The lowest price

Between these points are a constant flow of what are called *bids and offers* – investors willing to buy (bid) for shares and investors willing to sell (offer).

The following sections examine pricing, more specifically bids and offers, because bids and offers create a working market and the prices at which investors exchange ownership of shares. Furthermore, bids and offers and the high, low, open and close of a stock provide information that traders and quantitative analysts use to analyse price movements. This information is also often used to build trading algorithms for high frequency traders. Don't forget that bids and offers also act as a pricing benchmark for dark pools.

Grasping how pricing works

The markets are all about price. A buyer wants as low a price as possible and a seller as high a price as possible. The whole market is structured to constantly find a price that both the buyer and seller will agree on. Grasping the mechanics of pricing is crucial to understanding dark pools. Because dark pools don't display their prices, those who trade in them need some point of reference, which is why the old-fashioned displayed stock markets remain so important.

Dark pools use the prices from the displayed markets as a reference for their own pricing. The aim is to always provide an equal or better price for all participants than what is available on a displayed stock exchange.

For a trade to happen, the person willing to buy and the person willing to sell have to agree on a price. To come up with a price level, the stock exchanges came up with an ingenious, yet simple way to have an ongoing auction. Investors placed orders stating at what price and how much they were willing to buy or sell, and these were posted for everyone to see on a stock exchange. The investors who are willing to buy are said to be *bidding* for a stock, so their price suggestions became known as *bids*. The term bid in regards to stock trading is the price someone is willing to buy. The price at which a seller is willing to sell is called an *offer* (also sometimes referred to as an *ask*). A slight price difference between the best bid and the best offer – the best bid being lower and the best offer being higher – is called the *spread*.

On a trading book the highest price that someone is willing to buy the shares at is known as the *best bid*. The best bid guarantees the highest possible price for the stock for any seller coming to the market at that particular time. The lowest possible price a seller is willing to sell at is called the *best offer*, which guarantees a buyer the lowest possible price at that particular time. This mechanism of best bid and best offer is a great way to keep the market fair. It's planned as a way to give an investor the best possible price. Even if an order comes in for a price that is worse than the current available price on the market, an investor should always get the better price available.

The following table looks at bids and offers in action in the current real-time market. On the far left and right is the *size*, which is the amount of shares bid or offered. The top bid is the highest price someone is willing to *buy* the shares at, and the top offer is the lowest price someone is willing to *sell* the shares at.

Size	Bid	Offer	Size
200	50.09	50.10	1,000
1,000	49.95	50.15	200
7,000	49.90	50.20	8,000
3,000	49.85	50.25	500
500	49.80	50.30	1,000

Look at this table and assume that it displays the current live market order book. Because you don't have real-time access, your price information has a 15-minute delay. Therefore you can't be sure of the current price. You've decided that the maximum you'll pay is $50.20 and you want to buy 100 shares. Now remember that in a fair and properly working market you, as the buyer, would receive the lowest offer. In this case, unbeknownst to you the lowest offer is $0.10 lower than your limit, which is a good thing for you because you get the shares at a lower price. So if a better price is available on offer in the market, even though you were willing to pay more, the system of best bid and best offer would guarantee you the better price.

In a dark pool you wouldn't see any of this. If the trade was done through a dark pool and there was a willing seller in the pool, you should have your trade executed at the lowest offer equal to that in the displayed market (remember dark pools take their pricing reference from the displayed market). You could even have your trade executed at the midpoint between the displayed market's bid or offer.

Because you had chosen not to pay for a real-time price feed from your broker, you had a 15-minute delay on your market feed so you couldn't be sure of the exact price at that moment. You wanted to buy 100 shares and the highest price you wanted to pay for those shares was $50.20. You place your limit order and (in a fair market) you get the best offer (remember you're buying, so you pay the offer), which is $0.10 lower than your limit. The system of best bid and best offer guarantees you the best available price at that moment in time, even if you were willing to pay a higher price.

By always having a best bid and a best offer, even if an order comes into the market that is at a worse price than the best bid or offer, the order will be executed at the better price.

Looking at opening and closing prices

When trading begins at an exchange, including dark pools, the price that the first trade is executed at is the *opening* price. The last matched price of the day when the exchange closes is the *closing* price. These prices are important data points when analysing a stock's movements because they often act as resistance and support points for a stock. All analysts and traders use this data along with algorithmic trading programs, which use this data going back years and even decades.

The previous day's closing price is not necessarily the same as today's opening price. News flow during the time that the exchange is closed can influence the next day's opening price. Many companies, for example, release quarterly results after the market has closed; these results can affect orders coming in overnight to the order book. When the market opens, there might be a large imbalance in orders either to sell or to buy, causing the price of the stock to open either higher or lower than the previous day's close. When these orders are matched when trading opens, the price can vary from the previous day's close.

Analysts are particularly interested in the differences between the daily open and the daily close, and also the difference between the previous day's close and the next day's open. Within this information they can find possible ideas for trading strategies.

Looking at the highest and lowest prices

The highest and lowest prices of a day are one part of the determiner in what the range of the trading day will be. Just like the opening and closing price of a day, this data of the highest to lowest price is important to analysts. The *daily range* of a stock is the difference between its highest and lowest prices of the day. Analysts look closely at these points, and algorithmic trading programs often use them as a basis for sending orders into the market.

The daily range is part of calculating how much a stock's price can swing, more commonly referred to as *volatility*. Volatility is used in many stock valuation calculations, and it's also an indicator of risk. Abnormal volatility is always sure to fire off algorithmic trading programs because many of them trade based on a stock's volatility.

Daily high and low prices are some of the most important metrics in algorithmic trading. You will often see activity in a stock kick in when a stock's price is around its daily high or daily low. One of the reasons is that the high and low price points are often used to place stop-loss orders or for other traders as a price to enter a trade, depending on a trader's investment strategy, of course. When the price comes anywhere near a high or a low of the day, you'll see an increase in the amount of trades.

Because trading happens in milliseconds, don't just think of the high and low as a daily number, although that's what newspapers and other media sources quote. Algorithmic trading programs can and do split the highs and lows into much smaller increments, including hours, minutes and seconds. The timeframe used for highs and lows depends on the trading strategy; it's then compared to the stock's average range in the equivalent timeframe. Any deviation from the norm is commonly a trigger for a trading decision.

Making Buying and Selling Easier: Liquidity

When I discuss liquidity in markets, I'm not referring to water or any other form of liquid. The term, however, does give a great mental picture of what you're looking for. *Liquidity* in its basic financial form means the ease with which you can buy or sell whatever it is you want to buy or sell.

Liquidity is about volume; the more shares available to be bought and sold in the market, the more liquid a market is said to be. Another sign of liquidity is if when existing orders are taken out new ones come into the market to replenish them. Think of gushing whitewater rapids, but instead of water a constant torrent of new orders – both buy and sell and at different prices – comes into the market. Markets in general like liquidity, which is considered as decreasing risk, because it makes entering or exiting a trade easy.

All markets need liquidity, both displayed stock exchanges and dark pools. Liquidity is their lifeblood. Without it, trades can't be matched.

Liquidity also tends to have a very important effect on markets. Liquidity decreases spreads, which is the price difference between the bid and the offer. The more there are shares being offered and bid, the closer the bid and offer will come, which is good for investors because the spread between the bid and offer is what the investor (more often than not) pays; it's a cost to the investor.

When you sell a stock if you want to do the trade immediately, you receive the bid (which is lower than the offer). When you want to buy a stock immediately, you pay the offer (which is higher than the bid). In this way you always lose the difference of the spread. That's a cost you pay for immediate execution. So for an investor smaller spreads are good because they mean smaller costs.

However, liquidity isn't always what it seems. There are three types of liquidity:

- Market liquidity
- Off-market liquidity
- Phantom liquidity

The following sections explain in more depth market and off-market liquidity and why they're important. Refer to the nearby sidebar for more about phantom liquidity, which is a newer term and has caused plenty of debate.

Phantom liquidity: Does it exist or not?

Phantom liquidity is a concept that has come about with high frequency trading (HFT) and refers to the appearance of liquidity. If you look at an order book on a stock exchange, you'll see plenty of bids and offers and lots of volume on both sides of the trading book, but is the volume really there? If those bids and offers are posted by HFT programs, they can be withdrawn in milliseconds, which means that liquidity that appears to be there can disappear faster than the eye can blink. Is that real liquidity or is it phantom? Is it just meant to look like it is there but when you try to go for it, it disappears?

Supporters of HFT say there's no such thing as phantom liquidity; it's just a super-fast market. Those who oppose HFT say phantom liquidity is a serious problem and often cite the flash crash of 2010 as an example of phantom liquidity, when in just a few seconds the markets crashed several hundred points when liquidity was withdrawn. Chapter 13 discusses the flash crash of 2010 in greater detail.

Market liquidity

The volume you see posted in the trade book that's coming in and going out on an exchange is *market liquidity*. It's available to everyone to see, and it's the traditional form of liquidity. You can easily ascertain the liquidity of a stock from its market liquidity. Market liquidity is important because the more liquidity there is, the less effect a single order or a handful of orders has on the price of a stock. When there is plenty of liquidity, the value of the stock won't be overly affected by a single order.

To determine whether a stock has abundant market liquidity, pay special attention to the following:

- **Spread:** A small spread, even $0.01, indicates good liquidity.
- **Market depth:** Volume, in other words, the amount of shares on offer on both sides of the trading book, determines *market depth*.

  If plenty of shares (counted in the thousands or even tens of thousands) are on offer on both sides then that's an indication of good liquidity. Most orders nowadays are executed in lots of a few hundred shares; if there is liquidity far above that then these small orders won't move the markets. Also look for the order book to replenish with new volume when existing orders are taken out; so when a trade is matched and it disappears from the order book, are there new orders popping up on the screen?

  Market liquidity is important for dark pools also. If the pools themselves don't have liquidity, trades won't be executed, but liquidity is also important for dark pools from a pricing perspective. Dark pools take their price reference from the displayed market; the more liquidity there is, the tighter the spreads tend to be. The spreads in dark pools will follow those in the displayed markets.

One aspect of market liquidity is the *unseen liquidity*, which comes in the form of orders that show only part of the full order and replenish whenever a small part is fulfilled. For example, an order of 10,000 shares can be broken up into smaller parts that show only 200 on the order book. Every time the 200 shares are matched, another 200 will be posted to the order book until the full 10,000 is filled. Although this hidden liquidity doesn't show on the trading book, it's part of market liquidity.

Liquidity that is unseen may give the appearance of low liquidity; a stock maybe shows just 200 shares offered, but in reality behind it is an order for 20,000 that simply shows 200 shares at a time. The appearance of a lack of liquidity may cause some traders to try to execute orders on a dark pool or several dark pools, thus the order on the displayed market doesn't get executed, even if a counterparty was interested.

Off-market liquidity

Off-market liquidity isn't posted on the exchange. Basically, *off-market liquidity* consists of orders sent to a dark pool or a verbal (non-binding) order given to a broker to see whether he can find a match. The more there's off-market liquidity, the less accurate the displayed market price is as an indicator of fair value because much of the information about what price market participants are willing to trade at will not be known to all market participants. All liquidity in dark pools is regarded as off-market liquidity. Finding out how much off-market liquidity is available is a much harder task than working out market liquidity. This is where algorithmic trading comes into play.

Dark pools don't show how much volume is on offer. (They wouldn't be very dark otherwise, would they?) Off-market liquidity is in fact the main thing that makes dark pools *dark*; it's that inability to see how much is being offered or bid at any given time.

If you choose to invest in dark pools, you have to be a bit savvier about discovering the level of liquidity in a dark pool. To do so, use various algorithms and send small orders into a dark pool to test whether an order gets matched. An order getting matched confirms that there is at least an equal amount of volume in the market for that particular order, but there could also be much more available. If the order comes back cancelled then nothing is there. Sending out these kinds of test balloons helps algorithms find bigger orders, and then you can trade accordingly based on the information they have gathered.

Understanding the Importance of Market Makers

Market makers make sure that there is a constant availability of stocks to both buyers and sellers. Both the displayed (lit) markets and dark pools have market makers. Market makers (in general) provide liquidity. Anybody can provide liquidity, by simply placing a limit order on the market. A *limit order* is an order to buy or sell at a specific price. It then shows up on the stock exchange's order book or registers in a dark pool.

All investors who post limit orders, whether in the order book of a lit exchange or in a dark pool, provide liquidity. The orders that are executed against existing limit orders on the book are said to *take liquidity away*. Market participants have different reasons and strategies for investing and trading, with making money being the one common aspect.

The market makers are solely responsible for providing liquidity. Without existing levels of prices that other investors can trade with, there is no effective market. That is why market makers are so crucial to a working investment market.

Market makers provide both a bid and an offer price. When you want to sell, a market maker is willing to buy from you, and when you want to buy, a market maker is willing to sell to you. The market maker will make his money on the bid and offer difference, *the spread*, by selling a little higher than he is buying. The market maker takes on market risk, and for that risk his compensation is to make the spread.

Nowadays most market makers use some form of algorithmic trading model to automate their order processes, because a market maker is constantly updating his bids and offers. He commonly uses a benchmark price to decide the prices of his bids and offers and also the size of those orders.

As dark pools have emerged, and there are also many displayed stock markets, the importance of how and order is routed through all these different venues has become ever more important.

In this section, you'll see some of the tools the modern market maker uses when *making liquidity* (posting bids and offers). You'll also find out more about order routing and how and in what order orders are placed in the trading book. Because a market maker will often be on the opposite side of your trades, knowing how he goes about his business will help you in your own trading.

Using VWAP and MVWAP

A commonly used metric in algorithmic trading models is the volume weighted adjusted price (VWAP). Like its name suggests, it takes into account the volume of a stock during the trading period, which can be seconds, minutes, hours and so on.

The idea is pretty straightforward. If a stock can be bought at a price below the VWAP then it's a good price. If the price is above the VWAP then it's a bad price.

Market makers, big institutions and high frequency traders use the VWAP as a benchmark for their trading.

Check out this example to see the VWAP calculated. From the table, you can see that a stock has had four executed trades.

Price	Volume
15.50	1,000
16.00	500
15.75	2,000
15.80	200

To calculate the VWAP, do the following:

1. **Take the price of each trade and multiply it by the volume of that trade and add those results together.**

   In this case, $(15.50 \times 1,000) + (16.00 \times 500) + (15.75 \times 2,000) + (15.80 \times 200)$. The result is 58,160.

2. **Add all the volumes of the period in question:**

   $1,000 + 500 + 2,000 + 200 = 3,700$.

3. **Divide the price multiplied by volume total by the overall volume.**

   $58,160 \div 3,700 = 15.72$

Now you have the VWAP. You can then check the price at which you can currently buy the stock. If it's below 15.72 then it should be a good trade.

You can use the VWAP to build a moving volume weighted adjusted price or MVWAP. (You like all these acronyms?) MVWAP is a constantly updating metric of the VWAP. For example, say that you're using a one-minute VWAP. You can choose the number of references you want to have in your moving average. If you choose 20 then you simply take the last 20 VWAP results and calculate the average and keep updating this every minute.

The major difference between the VWAP and a MVWAP is that the traditional VWAP is calculated throughout the trading day and starts anew each trading day. The MVWAP, on the other hand, follows the timeframes that you've chosen and gives you a trailing VWAP, which evens out any sudden changes. On a normal trading day, trading is heavy at the open because orders build up throughout the night before the opening and are executed at the start of trading. This means that the early morning price has a big effect on VWAP for the total day. Using a MVWAP will even out this overweighting. With the need for constant updating and calculating, you can clearly see why the VWAP and the MVWAP are good benchmarks for algorithmic trading. With computer programs, orders can automatically be sent to the market based on VWAP and MVWAP calculations.

Getting to grips with order routing

As markets have become more and more complex, order routing has become a major factor in getting the best possible price. How your order is routed and what happens during the routing procedure are of major significance.

Before technology took over, you would call your broker, who would then call the trading floor, or perhaps another broker, and your order would be executed. Getting confirmation took minutes or at best tens of seconds. Now, with direct market access and fast computer algorithms trades are executed in milliseconds. Despite the increase in speed, the number of events that happen en route from placing your order to receiving a confirmation back has increased.

Understanding what happens during this process is important. The routing procedure can separate a bad broker from a good broker, and even possibly a dishonest broker from an honest one. Many of the issues and concerns regarding market structure, dark pools and HFT are related to order routing and it's therefore at the heart of the good versus evil debate surrounding HFT and dark pools.

When you place an order into the market, many things can and do happen. If you don't have direct market access, your order will first go to your broker. That order is often then routed to a dark pool in an attempt to find a matching order to trade against. If a matching order isn't found, the order will return to your broker and then will be sent to a lit stock exchange.

The process of routing an order, although usually automated and probably happening in milliseconds, still takes time. As the order goes from one venue to another, information is leaking and there are algorithms programmed to find information on orders and trade against those. So as your order moves around the different venues, there is the possibility that faster traders (algorithms) will move the price based on information leakage.

Focusing on price/time priority

Traditionally, orders that have come into the market have been placed in what is called *price/time priority*, which means that the best price is always first in line – the lowest price possible for the buyer and the highest price possible for the seller. For orders of equal price, the orders that have come in first are ahead in the queue for that price. Refer to Chapter 8 for additional information about price/time priority.

This is still the way the market is supposed to work, but in the modern market the concept of price/time priority has been tested to its limits. In fact, how well it's been adhered to in question. Certain types of orders in some exchanges allow market participants to jump the queue in effect. Special order types are complex orders with many attributes; they act in a specific way, depending on other orders in the order book and what orders are executed. These orders often aren't understood or known by many market participants and their execution also requires the use of algorithmic trading models. You can read about special order types in Chapter 9.

Eyeing direct market access

Direct market access allows a trader or investor control over the routing of his order. With the abundance of dark pools and displayed stock exchanges to choose from, having the ability to directly access those you want gives you much more control over your trading activities. Professional and active traders primarily use direct market access. With direct market access, a trader can bypass the broker and place an order with more speed to the exchange that the trader wants.

High frequency traders actively use direct market access because they need to be able to route an order in a fraction of a second via an algorithm with endless combinations.

The overall cost of direct market access to the investor can be seen in the decreased cost of commissions. Because there is no need for a middleman and the investor controls the trade routing, commissions are smaller, although there's normally a minimum demand for trading activity when it comes to direct market access services.

If direct market access allows for faster execution with smaller commissions then why doesn't everyone want direct market access?

For a retail investor, it can be a question of activity. If the investor doesn't trade regularly, the minimum costs for getting direct market access can be prohibitive. The most important factor for anyone using direct market access is the knowledge and control of how orders are routed. With direct market access the investor may be faced with many decisions, such as what special order types to use and what exchanges to route the trade to. Should he exclude some or not? What about using dark pools? With the use of direct market access comes more complexity. The investor needs to know the different kinds of market venues inside out and also needs to have expertise in the use of special order types. With direct market access making an order can actually become a laborious affair.

Part II
Diving into Dark Pool Markets

Top five ways to knowing who's who in the dark pool markets

- ✔ **Shine a floodlight on dark pools.** By knowing what types of people and what types of institutions operate in dark pools you'll have a good overview of how dark pools work.

- ✔ **Strengthen your knowledge of the influencers.** Each dark pool influencer affects the evolution of the market. Understand what the influence is and you'll understand how things will develop in the future.

- ✔ **Develop your legal knowledge.** Examine the legislative landscape of dark pools — the foundation of the market.

- ✔ **Remember the culprits.** A dark pool can be a predatory environment. Many operators have been fined for suspicious behaviour. Know who they are.

- ✔ **Make the best of your dip in a dark pool.** You're also a player in a dark pool, willing or unwilling. Educate yourself as to who does what in a dark pool and invest with more confidence.

 Get more information on recognising the actions you can take to make sure that you get the best out of a dark pool transaction at www.dummies.com/extras/darkpools.

In this part . . .

- ✔ Meet all the major players in the dark pool markets and see how they go about swimming in dark pools.

- ✔ Cultivate your knowledge of the regulations that act as the foundation to dark pools and what changes are in the works.

- ✔ Discover the different providers that provide the dark pool venues and the subtle differences that separate them from each other.

- ✔ Discover how you can stop yourself becoming the prey of predatory dark pool operators and know who those operators might be.

Chapter 4

Introducing Dark Pool Providers

Dark pools are a major part of the global financial markets. They're an alternative place to trade stocks to that of a traditional stock exchange. Big institutions needed places where they could buy large amounts of stock without tipping their hand to other investors and so moving the price of the stock. Brokers and banks were also keen on setting up their own dark pools so they could then internally match trades and not have to go to the stock exchanges and pay the stock exchange fees.

The dark pool market is vast and different banks and brokers offer many different types of dark pools. You need to know the differences between the various dark pool providers, because each has its own specific way of operating and executing trades, which can affect how your trade is settled.

Dark pools are under constant media and regulatory scrutiny, and several have been fined or are under investigation. Some providers have taken liberties with their client orders and trading information, and that means you're at risk. Make sure you know which dark pools have been fined and which ones are under investigation to protect your investments as much as possible. If you don't know the good guys from the bad guys, you may well end up paying for it when you trade.

I don't list all the dark pools in this chapter, because globally there are too many to list. New ones are popping up and old ones are being shut down all the time. In fact, dark pools are an always-moving market. I focus on some of the better known dark pools – basically, the major players – so you can get a handle on their main differences and at least stick your big toe into the pool, if you so desire.

Comparing the Different Types of Dark Pool Providers

You may be surprised to discover that dark pools, for the most part, offer similar offerings, although some differences do exist. They all promise the *deepest liquidity*, the best execution with the minimum impact on price, sometimes in what appears to be exactly the same language. It's a miracle they get any business at all, because differentiating one from the other is so hard.

One thing that many of the major dark pools have in common is that a large number of them have received big fines from regulators and/or are currently under investigation by regulators, which tells you of the state of the current market. Many traders, fund managers and investors have a widespread distrust of dark pools and what goes on in them because of recent events, and rightly so. Some providers have been very naughty indeed. That's why you need to be very vigilant about which dark pools your broker uses to execute your trades. (Refer to Chapter 15 for ways that you can keep tabs on your trades.)

This constant regulatory scrutiny also foresees further legislation and further consolidation in the industry. More than likely, some dark pools will shut down or a larger dark pool will buy them. The cost of consistently doing battle with regulators in a market that isn't growing will be the death of many dark pools. (Chapter 6 discusses in greater depth some of the regulatory challenges that dark pools face and what they mean to you.)

These sections discuss the main types of dark pools and how they differ from each other in the way that they execute your trades. As technology and the demands of investors and traders have changed, dark pools have evolved with new ways of executing trades.

Big-time investments: Block-oriented dark pools

Block-oriented dark pools are the old school representatives of dark pools. They're what dark pools were originally designed for – matching large blocks of shares among big investors with the minimum of market price impact.

The amounts of shares involved aren't small, like lot shares of a 100 or so; block-oriented dark pools often have a minimum block size in the tens of thousands of shares. Because of the minimum share requirements, these dark pools are relatively free of high frequency traders who prefer to trade in smaller 100- and 200-share lots.

If you're a private investor, these dark pools are probably out of your reach because of the minimum share size. However, if you represent an institutional trader, you'll definitely want access to these types of dark pools because they can provide you with large pools of liquidity, which is just what you need.

They also have a downside: finding a match to your order can be difficult. The bigger the size (amount of shares) of your order, the harder it will be to find a single matching order. As a result, block-oriented dark pools can become a problem because they may not be able to find matching orders with enough volume.

No minimum shares required: Streaming liquidity pools

As dark pool providers have been looking to grow, streaming liquidity pools have become more popular. *Streaming liquidity pools* don't have a minimum share requirement so they have opened the doors to high frequency traders in the hope that the high frequency traders bring liquidity to the pools.

Streaming dark pools offer the possibility of finding a matching trade because they allow smaller traders in. These different orders can be batched together to make a matching trade with a larger single order.

The risk with a streaming liquidity pool is information leakage. High frequency traders use small orders to sniff out larger orders. If high frequency traders are successful in determining the larger orders, they'll push the price against you and you'll get your trade filled at a worse price.

If you're worried about predatory high frequency traders then having your trades routed to a streaming liquidity pool is a sure way to come face to face with the high frequency traders. Currently, these pools are the most popular types of dark pools. Because high frequency traders are present in these markets, they may appear to have deep pools of liquidity.

Crossing pools

Crossing pools are defined by how they match trades – an important factor for any client in a dark pool. A *cross* is simply when a broker receives both a buy and a sell order for the same price, and she can then match the orders against each other. When you're making a trade, you're always looking for the best possible cross, either at your limit or preferably even better.

When your trade is being executed in a dark pool, you're looking to have your trade executed at the midpoint of the spread and to not have the price of the stock move against you immediately after the execution of your trade. (Chapter 2 explains the midpoint.)

The three main types of crossing pool are

- ✔ **Scheduled cross pools:** A *scheduled cross* is a bit like an old-fashioned silent auction. Orders are submitted to the pool, and at a predetermined time the orders that have been sent in are matched. In this way the pool tries to gather as much liquidity as possible. The fact that the bids and offers are sent in and then matched at a predetermined time means that price impact, while trying to find liquidity, can be minimised. The schedule of the crossing is based on the rules of the individual dark pool; it can be every few minutes or it can be in hours.

- ✔ **Continuous cross pools:** This is the most common type of dark pool. As the name implies, *continuous cross pools*, sometimes referred to as *lit stock exchange*, are similar to a traditional stock exchange. Orders are continuously executed as and when there is a matching order in the market.

- ✔ **Hybrid markets:** *Hybrid markets* have specialised structures of how they match their trades. For example, they may be based on a benchmark, such as Volume Weight Adjusted Price (VWAP), which is a common price benchmark used by traders and market makers that takes into account the price of a stock based on its trading volume over a set period of time. You can find out more about VWAP and how it is calculated and used in Chapter 11.

Looking at Bank- and Broker-Owned Providers

There are dozens of dark pool providers all over the world. Most major banks have their own dark pool, which they own and run. Banks use their own dark pools primarily to match internal orders but also to compete for business from outside of the bank. In addition, major banks use several of the independent banks for their own trading and as a venue to match their clients' trades. I introduce you to the major ones in these sections.

Barclays LX Liquidity Cross

Barclays Capital owns and runs LX Liquidity Cross, which has grown at a fast rate. Launched in 2009, it was for a time the biggest dark pool in the United States. In fact, no other dark pool traded as large a volume of trades as Barclays LX. That was until the New York attorney general slapped it with a lawsuit accusing it of fleecing its clients and letting them be ripped apart by predatory high frequency traders.

According to the New York state attorney, Barclays LX had promised its clients that it scrutinised and risk rated all the traders in its dark pool for predatory trading behaviour and would allow the clients the choice to opt out of trading with those traders the client didn't want to trade with. The lawsuit claims that Barclays in fact didn't do as it promised and went even further in actively allowing high frequency traders to trade against its clients.

Unlike some dark pool providers Barclays chose to publicly publish its trading volume data on a regular basis. In this respect Barclays wasn't that dark.

Barclays LX aims to build trust among clients and limit flow toxicity by allowing its clients to choose the type of flow that their orders transact with. By providing clients with reports on trade flow within the Barclays LX pool and by analysing its trade flow Barclays hopes to spot any attempts at gaming the market.

Barclays ranks orders in several categories that are based on the type of liquidity they provide, such as aggressive or passive types of liquidity. Barclays refers to this practice as *liquidity profiling*. Characteristics used include price movements in favour of a trade within a second of execution, order size and how active the trader is at providing against taking liquidity.

The client can then choose what type of provider she wants to interact with, thereby avoiding predatory liquidity that may increase the overall cost of execution.

Barclays LX prioritises executions based on three categories:

- **Price:** The best price will go to the front of the line.
- **Tier:** Barclays would place its client orders into a tier system with four tiers. The first is client orders, which is followed by broker dealers.

  The tiers are based on four factors in order of priority:

    - Tier 1: Barclays' own order flow.
    - Tier 2: Order flow from third-party broker dealers.
    - Tier 3: Barclays' principal order flow.
    - Tier 4: Principal order flows from third-party broker dealers.

- **Time of order receipt:** If an order came in for the same price and from the same tier, the order that came in first would be prioritised and placed ahead in the queue.

In a situation when there is a seller at the *bid* price and a buyer at the *offer* price, Barclays splits the price advantage on an 80/20 split in favour of the liquidity provider versus the liquidity taker. A liquidity provider is a market maker that offers both a bid and an offer at a limit price. The aim of doing so is to provide both participants with a better price than what they were willing to take.

For example, the market for SPY is $152.05/$152.06. Client A provides liquidity with a limit order to buy at the offer price (buy at $152.06). An order comes in from Client B to sell at the bid (sell at $152.05).

Client A is posted to buy .01 above the bid, creating a spread overlap of .01.

80 per cent of the spread goes to Client A who is providing liquidity: 80 per cent × .01 = .008.

20 per cent of the spread goes to Client B who is taking liquidity: 20 per cent × .01 = .002.

The trade executes at $152.052.

Therefore, Client A buys at $152.052 instead of $152.06, resulting in $0.008 of price improvement. Client B sells at $152.052 instead of $152.05, resulting in $0.002 of price improvement.

Barclays LX also provides some VIP clients with the facility to use the bank's money to execute an order.

The pool has more than 550 participants. About 40 per cent of clients are internal trading desks, 35 per cent are Barclays Capital electronic trading clients and the remaining 25 per cent are various outside brokers.

Barclays gives priority of orders to its own internal clients. Although dark pools are meant for trading large blocks of shares, just like many other dark pools that allow algorithmic trading, Barclays LX trade sizes are an average of 300 shares with more than 135 million shares being traded daily.

To improve liquidity Barclays LX works with other dark pool providers such as UBS, Credit Suisse, ITG, Citadel and KCG (the merged entity of Knight and GETCO).

CrossFinder

CrossFinder was the biggest US dark pool until Barclays LX surpassed it in terms of traded volume in 2013. It again became the biggest when the New York attorney general slapped Barclays LX with a lawsuit. The Swiss bank Credit Suisse now owns CrossFinder.

Whereas Barclays LX chose to become more transparent, CrossFinder has decided to go the other way and become darker. In 2013 it decided to stop voluntarily publishing volume data from its dark pool. This could've just been a business decision, because Barclays LX dark pool was catching up and CrossFinder didn't want to be seen as coming in second to its biggest competitor. CrossFinder's decision to stop publishing data increased suspicions around the whole dark pool industry and was seen as a sign of dark pools becoming even more opaque.

CrossFinder promises to 'minimise impact and maximise execution quality' and lists as its advantages the ability of trading at or within the spread and not showing any of the order on the order book. Basically, the promise to do what all other dark pools promise to do. So nothing spectacularly new there.

Fidelity Capital Markets

Fidelity is a giant among world financial services providers; it's perhaps best known for its mutual funds. Fidelity offers two different dark pools: CrossStream, its original dark pool, and in 2013 Fidelity opened a second dark pool called BLOX.

CrossStream

The CrossStream dark pool started in 2006 and aims to use the large internal trade flow of Fidelity to match trades anonymously. CrossStream makes use of algorithms to match trades and also offers a wide range of order types for clients to be able to take control of the order execution. Any services involving algorithms and special order types tend to be venues where high frequency traders operate, so if you want to avoid high frequency traders then CrossStream is probably a venue you don't want to trade in.

BLOX

BLOX, which stands for Block Liquidity Opportunity Cross, was launched in 2013. It was set up to match anonymously larger block trades; in other words, trades in excess of 10,000 shares. In the beginning BLOX started off as an experiment with about a dozen institutional investors involved. Later, CrossStream grew the pool to include more investors. It promises a safe trading environment for larger block trades executing at the midpoint of the best bid and offers a standard practice for dark pools.

The fact that Fidelity felt there was a need and a demand for a dark pool specialising in block trades is indicative that the original CrossStream dark pool allows market participants who run high frequency trading (HFT) programs. Fidelity hasn't confirmed this, but what other possible reason would there be for another dark pool from the same company?

BLOX also promises to monitor the traders in its pool for predatory behaviour and thus protect those who trade in its dark pool. BLOX uses all kinds of fancy words on its promotional material to back up this claim. These promises are very similar to the ones that Barclays LX made, only to have Barclays receive a lawsuit accusing it of exactly the same type of tactics. Until clear legislation and legal precedents are set for how dark pools protect participants, be very sceptical of any promises by a dark pool provider regarding protecting you from *toxic flow* – which is just another term for high frequency traders.

GETCO/KCG

GETCO started as a proprietary trading firm, and the name is synonymous with algorithmic trading. However, since the company purchased Knight Capital Group, the name of GETCO is on the way out and KCG is the official name going forward. The company set up its own dark pool, called GETCO Execution Services, which claims to source liquidity for clients and execute trades with minimum price impact.

GETCO aims to use its algorithmic capabilities in its dark pool to find the best execution for its clients' trades. If your trades are being routed through GETCO Execution Services, you'll find that a major part of the counterparties in your trades are high frequency traders.

Sigma X

One of the biggest dark pools established in 2006 is Sigma X, which Goldman Sachs runs. Sigma X has recently had some problems and has been one of those dark pools adding to the concerns around the alternative trading landscape.

The Financial Industry Regulatory Authority (FINRA), which oversees dark pools, fined Sigma X $800,000 for not executing its client orders correctly. So Sigma X is another naughty dark pool operator.

Hundreds of thousands of trades were found to have been executed at the wrong price. The FINRA's report found that Sigma X had traded through protected quotes. In the United States, the best bid and the best offer (regardless of which lit venue they're on) are *protected*, meaning that the trade should be executed at the protected venue first, unless of course a better price can be obtained for both parties (meaning a transaction within the spread). Sigma X had executed client trades at prices inferior to the National Best Bid Offer (NBBO) price. One of its clients spotted the discrepancy and lodged a complaint.

In its defence Sigma X blamed a slow feed that didn't update the NBBO in a timely manner and it said it has since fixed the problem. (Refer to Chapter 9 for more information on the NBBO.)

The fact that prices were executed at an inferior price raises concerns about *front running*, which is when someone, often a broker or other trader, receives information of an incoming order and trades before the incoming order gets to the market with some market participants who suspect that it wasn't an accident, but in fact business as usual for Goldman Sachs.

Whatever the truth is behind the debate, Sigma X's fine caused reputational damage to Goldman's dark pool and there is speculation that Goldman may even shut down Sigma X.

ConvergEx

ConvergEx is the dark pool owned by the Bank of New York Mellon. ConvergEx has two dark pools:

- ✔ **VortEx:** VortEx allows direct market access and algorithmic trading.
- ✔ **ConvergEx Cross:** ConvegrEx Cross is for block trades with a minimum of 10,000 shares and tries to supply large block trades with minimal price impact.

ConvergEX promises not to trade against clients and claims that it's 'always focused on best execution by remaining neutral and not competing with liquidity or order providers'. However, ConvergEx suffered a serious reputational setback when in 2013 it admitted to having 'fleeced' some of its clients. ConvergeEx was fined nearly $150 million for overcharging some of its clientele.

What ConvergEx did was route trades through an affiliate in Bermuda for clients that it didn't expect to notice – all in all, a very naughty and devious tactic. As a result, according to the *Financial Times* some large institutions stopped routing trades through ConvergEx. ConvergeEx is still trying to recover from the setback. One comfort is that so many dark pools are facing fines that at least ConvergeEx isn't alone.

ConvergeEx does have one of the best morning briefings available. Written by its chief market strategist, Nicholas Colas, it's always an enlightening and amusing read. If you can get on the mailing list, you'll never be bored again reading financial marketing material.

Alpha Y

Societe Generale's dark pool Alpha Y came to the market a little later than most, as recently as 2013. From the onset it made clear that it uses algorithms to improve liquidity and order matching. Like so many other dark pool providers, it also promises to protect investors from predatory high frequency traders, and it claims to do this via the use of algorithms that detect such traders. If it has algorithms to detect high frequency traders then it's logical to infer that it also allows high frequency traders into its dark pool.

Societe Generale's pitch is its expertise in derivatives, saying that its algorithmic abilities from its derivative side have been put to use in Alpha Y to improve execution for its clients.

DBA/Super X

Deutsche Bank has two dark pools, DBA for its European operations and Super X for its US operations. Like so many other dark pools, they're currently under investigation by US regulators.

Unlike with many other dark pools, Deutsche Bank has been more transparent with its Super X pool. It has published a Q&A about what types of orders it allows and how it matches orders. You can find the Q&A at the Deutsche Markets website (`https://autobahn.db.com/microSite/docs/SuperX_FAQ_v17.pdf`).

Deutsche Bank promises that its algorithms and smart order routers adapts 'the execution of trades to all available dark and displayed venues'. Like all dark pools, its marketing material goes into very little detail of how actual orders are handled and what the real benefits are to the clients.

Looking at Exchange-Owned Providers

The dark pools established by banks and brokers have taken business away from the traditional lit exchanges. To counteract this loss of business, the exchanges have chosen a 'if you can't beat them, join them' attitude and started setting up their own dark pools. Remember, exchanges have been doing this since the beginning. Larger block trades would often be negotiated and agreed to outside of exchange hours and then be executed the next day at the agreed price, when markets opened. As the new dark pools competed for the business of the stock exchanges, the stock exchanges began setting up their own sophisticated dark pools with many of the same attributes as their new competitors.

The new exchange-owned dark pools act exactly in the same way as other dark pools. Investors who want to execute their trades in the dark now have the option of an exchange-owned provider as well without having to go to a banker- or broker-provided dark pool. At least, that's what the following dark pools hope for anyway.

International Securities Exchange (ISE)

The International Securities Exchange (ISE) was the first lit market to provide a dark pool in 2006, which it called MidPointMatch. Like any other dark pool, it claims better liquidity and better speed and competitive pricing. From the beginning ISE gave access to algorithmic trading in its dark pool. It allows its clients to interact either in the dark through its dark pool or in the displayed market.

ISE doesn't have a minimum block requirement and, to its credit, it has been open about the fact that it courted algorithmic traders to its pool. This inevitably led to concerns about gaming and predatory HFT. ISE combated this by making it possible for clients to enter minimum quantity requirements in their orders. High frequency traders prefer to execute orders in small lots, so this minimum requirement was supposed to reduce interactions with high frequency traders for those investors who wanted to avoid them. For example, a client could set a minimum quantity of 1,000 shares: this is an amount of shares that a high frequency trader is likely to use, and so the order wouldn't interact with a high frequency trader order.

New York Stock Exchange/Euronext

Two dark pools are represented here, one in the United States and the other in Europe. Here is a bit of information that can help you keep the two apart:

- ✔ **The New York Stock Exchange (NYSE):** The NYSE really does offer something a bit different when it comes to dark pools. It has a retail investor dark pool that doesn't allow algorithmic traders into its pool that it calls a *retail liquidity programme*. Although still small by volume standards, something you would expect for a retail pool, it has been chugging along nicely. If it does keep out the high frequency traders then retail investors should feel comfortable having their trades routed to this pool. But then again what's the point of such a pool? Retail investor orders tend not to have a market impact so what is the added value in having a dark pool?

✔ **SmartPool:** The European dark pool offers better liquidity with minimal price impact. You may have heard that claim before.

This dark pool has a comprehensive offering, including 15 exchanges in Europe, which pretty much covers the whole market. Like all exchange-owned dark pools, it claims better execution thanks to the multiple sources that trade in its displayed exchanges. According to Euronext, it can achieve a 'price improvement of between 4 to 6 basis points per trade in blue chip securities'. This per cent doesn't sound like much, but when trading large volumes it can be a significant gain.

BATS Global Markets

In 2013, two major global exchanges, BATS and Direct Edge, merged to make BATS Global Markets. Like so many other dark pools, BATS has been the subject of regulatory investigation focusing on accusations by whistle blowers that it provided unfair advantages to high frequency traders in its dark pools.

BATS president William O'Brien was a fierce defender of HFT as a positive market force. As a result, he had become the de facto face of the HFT proponents, although the company suddenly dropped him in 2014. The reasons are believed to have been related to the ongoing investigation.

O'Brien became famous when his CNBC debate with *Flash Boys* author Michael Lewis and IEX director Brad Katsuyama turned into a heated argument and then went viral. You can view this piece of dark pool history on YouTube at www.youtube.com/watch?v=RcpmHyPD_PY.

The investigation into BATS and Direct Edge has centred on the subjects addressed in this book. It is believed that BATS special order types didn't interact with the market in the way the company had promised some clients they would. This made it possible for some participants (high frequency traders) to take advantage of other BATS clients. The regulators are saying BATS aided in this endeavour.

Direct Edge has gone someway into opening up its special order types and produced a comprehensive package explaining the different special order types it provides. Although it concerns only the special order types offered by Direct Edge, it's actually a very good primer into special order types in general. You can find it on the Direct Edge website at www.directedge.com.

BATS is also the owner of Chi-X Europe, which shouldn't be confused with the independent dark pool provider Chi-X Global. BATS acquired Chi-X Europe in 2011, and it's a direct competitor to the Euronext dark pool, trading across 15 European markets.

Eyeing Some Providers That Have Been Bought Out

A few other dark pools were originally independent, although bigger banks have since bought them. They remain active and continue to be important in the world of dark pools.

Chi-X Global

Chi-X Global is of the major global dark pools. Calling it independent is perhaps stretching it a bit because a consortium of banks, including Goldman Sachs, Bank of America, Morgan Stanley and UBS, own it.

Chi-X Global is a very commonly used dark pool and is probably one of the venues your broker uses to execute your trades.

Instinet

Instinet isn't as independent as it used to be. Nomura acquired it in 2011. However, it has retained its independent nature, providing a global reach with its dark pool giving access to more than 60 countries.

Instinet divides its dark pools into the following geographical categories, offering different types of pools within each area:

✓ **United States:** In the United States, Instinet has several different dark pools, each one with a slightly different setup. The main ones are as follows:

- **VWAP Cross** provides a dark pool that is attractive to institutional investors and matches trades based on the VWAP benchmark.

- **CBX US** is as an equal access pool that operates on a strict time price priority, according to Instinet.

✔ **EMEA:** The acronym stands for Europe, the Middle East and Africa. The reality is that the Middle East and Africa are such small markets that the dark pool activity there is not noteworthy. Instinet has two main dark pools for Europe:

- **BlockMatch** is a block-specialising dark pool. Refer to the earlier section 'Big-time investments: Block-oriented dark pools' for more information about their characteristics.

- **VWAP Cross** is a European dark pool also based on the VWAP benchmark.

✔ **Asia Pacific:** In the Asia Pacific region Instinet has dark pools in Australia, Hong Kong and Japan. The main pools operating in that region are as follows:

- **Instinet BLX Australia** is a dark pool that specialises in matching larger block trades in Australia.

- **CBX Japan:** CBX Japan offers a commission-only, no-rebate and no-payment-for-order-flow dark pool.

- **CBX Hong Kong:** Like the CBX Japan dark pool, the Hong Kong pool also does not accept payment for order flow and nor does it offer rebates. Only a commission is charged, on executed trades.

Deep trouble with the SEC: Liquidnet

Liquidnet is another dark pool provider that faced a fine for nasty shenanigans. According to the SEC, Liquidnet didn't correctly protect client data when it allowed another business unit access to client trading data that was used to market new issues to clients based on how they had previously traded. For these transgressions Liquidnet was fined $2 million.

Like all dark pool providers, Liquidnet promised clients maximum anonymity and minimum price impact on their trades. It failed to deliver.

Liquidnet has a large pool of clients, with more than 700 asset managers using its pool. Liquidnet claims that the average size of a trade on its pools is 40,000 shares – 100 times larger than other exchanges. If this claim is true then Liquidnet really is a provider to large institutions.

Liquidnet is one of the original alternative trading venues and dark pools, having been set up as early as 2001 with 38 member firms and then growing to more than 700 today.

Chapter 5

Meeting the Players and Places

In This Chapter

▶ Introducing the market makers

▶ Checking out the venues where the action takes place

▶ Understanding who the different participants are

▶ Examining how the players operate

Chapter 3 describes how a securities market typically functions. One thing is certain: markets have come a long way from the days when traders met by a single bench and traded! Nowadays trading is a bit more complicated (although the principle remains the same). Today fast Internet connections, real time price quotes and a global market that is big – massive in fact – make trading quicker and easier. And the number of people involved in trading around the world is huge.

The larger a market gets, the more supporting structures it needs, and dark pools are no different. This chapter takes a closer look at all the participants and structures that keep dark pools trading and ticking along like a well-oiled machine (well, not always). Part IV discusses when things go bump in the trading world.

Recognising Who the Market Makers Are

The clue is in the name: a market maker's job is to *make the market*, which means a *market maker* always provides both an offer to sell and a bid to buy a certain stock at the same time. (Market makers are sometimes referred to as *specialists*.) The market maker makes money by buying and selling the *spread* (the difference between the bid and the offer). Basically, it's selling just a little bit higher than buying.

Market makers tend to cover only a handful of stocks, constantly buying and selling, buying and selling. Market makers are absolutely vital to a working securities market; they're the oil that greases the machine, because they're responsible for providing all that important liquidity. They make sure that for an investor looking to buy or sell a security there's always a price at which a deal can be done.

Market makers normally pay exchanges or venues a fee for the privilege of being a market maker. They have also flocked to dark pools, and dark pools need them just like an exchange does, simply for the liquidity they provide.

For market makers, a dark pool is just another venue to ply their trade.

They also turn over stocks at a breakneck pace. They're happy to pocket a penny here and a penny there per stock, constantly churning the stocks they cover, which is how they make a living. Market making is a business based on big volumes and savvy risk management.

Market making is by no means a risk-free business, especially because spreads are so tight. (A spread is said to be *tight* when the bid and the offer prices are very close to one and other. A spread is *wide* when the bid and offer prices are far apart.)

Market makers fall into two categories:

- Actual human beings, just like you and me.
- Computerised market makers that automatically make bids and offers based on a computer program.

Dark pool venues need both kinds of market makers so that trades can be executed and they can make a fee.

The following sections examine these two categories of market makers.

Heading towards extinction: The human touch

Many humans used to work as market makers, but the advancement of technology has made the human market maker a dying breed. Long gone are the days when big men in funny jackets stood in a pit screaming at each other and throwing bits of paper around. One by one, those kinds of open outcry market venues have closed.

The continuing trend has been towards computerised automation simply because computers can do the job much faster and much more accurately. Humans just can't compete on speed. They just aren't as quick as a computer program in placing an order. Humans can take several seconds to fill an order and press buy/sell, whereas a computer can do it in a fraction of a second. Humans are also prone to making mistakes; for example, buying when they should be selling. There's a popular term for erroneous trades: *fat finger trades*, which comes from tapping two keys at once, thus making a trade larger than originally intended. Fat fingers make for slow and inaccurate orders and computers don't have fingers.

Going the automated route

Automated market makers are computer algorithms that do exactly what human market makers do, but at an exceptionally fast, whirling pace. The pace at which they place bids and offers is calculated in fractions of a second, sometimes in a millionth of a second.

They use many of the same strategies as human market makers, but due to the sheer volume and speed that they can place orders at, spreads have become much tighter, as hundreds of different programs jockey for position and jump in front of each other in the order book, trying to make a trade only to immediately turn around and do the opposite. The aim always being to catch that all-important spread.

Examining the Venue: Where All the Action Takes Place

The venue is where all the institutions and people who trade on the markets come together to close their deals. It doesn't get more important than the venue. Without a place to trade, there would be no market. The trading venue is where it all happens. It's similar to an athletics stadium: the game takes place there with the spectators watching, the media following and reporting, the athletes participating and the officials facilitating the action.

Each trading venue has its own rules and ways of conducting trade. The structure and setting they provide makes (or at least should make) for an orderly and reliable place to conduct business for traders and investors. The following sections identify and then compare and contrast the two main types of venues in greater detail.

Knowing the venue options

No each trading venue is the same; they all have their own quirks and differences. There are rules, procedures and of course fees. For an investor, these differences can have a big effect on your investing bottom line. You should always know the basics of the venue you are trading in; it will help you to get the best out of all your trades. The main types of venues are as follows:

- ✔ **Traditional exchanges:** A traditional stock exchange is one where traders and investors congregate to buy and sell shares. Trading tends to be done in the open, so that orders sent to the market are shown publicly on an order book. You can see who is willing to sell or buy and at what price. If you're in a hurry, you can see at what price and of how much of a stock you can buy or sell at right at that moment. It's very similar to an auction, where traders and investors post bids (orders to buy) and offers (orders to sell) on the order book for all to see.

  A stock market was the traditional venue. If you've ever watched the financial news, you'll have seen footage from a stock market. Possibly the one you saw was the New York Stock Exchange. A stock market is a venue where buyers and sellers meet and transactions with stocks are done.

- ✔ **Alternative trading networks:** As technological innovations evolved, market participants began using the latest possible technology. Traditional stock markets were slow to adopt computerisation, and as a result alternative trading networks (ATNs) and electronic communication networks (ECNs) using computers were born. They were the forerunners of dark pools. Those who had access to ATNs could trade stocks, and in the early days there were many opportunities for *arbitrage* (making a profit from price differences of the same product in different markets). Because of their speed (pedestrian by today's standards), ATNs soon became competitors to traditional stock markets.

- ✔ **Off exchange venues:** They're dark pools by another name. When big institutions needed a place to trade where they could get better execution and didn't want to show the market all that they were planning to do, dark pools started to be set up. They have grown from strength to strength and now make up a major part of overall trading volume in the United States and in Europe.

Differentiating between stock markets and dark pools

Traditional stock markets are crucial to dark pools. Although stock markets could survive without dark pools, dark pools couldn't survive without stock markets. What differentiates stock markets from dark pools is that the stock markets are *transparent*, which means that the trading information and the amount of stocks that are bid and offered are available for everyone to see.

Because of their transparency, stock markets are often referred to as *lit* markets, which refer to the fact that they shine a light on what they're doing, unlike dark pools.

The reason stock markets play such a crucial role when it comes to dark pools is that the people who use dark pools also use stock markets, constantly looking for the best price at which they can do business. Stock markets are bigger in size than dark pools, and they play a major role in the market of producing prices for stocks. Stock markets are in fact the dark pools' biggest competitors.

Thanks to regulation designed to protect the investor regardless of which venue a stock is traded at, the buyer must always get the best offer price (the minimum for which someone is willing to part with his stock) and the seller the best bid price (the maximum somcone is willing to pay for the stock). This is to guarantee a fair market. This rule is referred to as the National Best Bid Offer (NBBO) and it's run by the NASDAQ.

When it comes to the rest of the world, dark pools are still a bit of a Wild West with regards to regulation. Europe in particular is racing to implement MiFID II, which includes legislation on how dark pool orders are transacted and reported. You can read more about the effects of legislation in Chapter 6.

On the other hand, dark pools are just as much at the centre of market activity as the traditional stock markets; all the major market participants also congregate in the dark pools. The traders, broker and dealers, market makers, banks, family offices and high frequency traders ply their trade in the multitude of different dark pool venues (in addition to the stock markets, of course). They all in one way or another utilise the fast data links and co-located servers that data centres provide. Each dark pool is slightly different, with its own rules and platforms. I talk more about the different types of dark pools in Chapter 4.

Stock markets: Moving from non-profit to profit

Stock markets used to be non-profit organisations. They were owned by the market makers, who were said to 'own a seat' on the exchange. Recently, stock markets have become for-profit corporations; most of them, like the New York Stock Exchange, have in fact themselves become stock exchange listed companies. That's right, the New York Stock Exchange is listed on the New York Stock Exchange.

The change from a non-profit to a for-profit business has caused much debate because stock markets have been allowed to keep their self-regulating organisation status even though they have become for-profit businesses. This means that they still make the rules and enforce them themselves. Because of the profit-making factor, many feel that it's a conflict of interest.

Identifying the Cast of Characters

Many different kinds of characters and participants play some sort of role in dark pools. This section introduces you to them all. These participants are also present in traditional displayed stock exchanges. Some individual participants may operate in only one or the other (dark pool or displayed exchange), but the terms can be found used in both markets.

Wherever you trade, it's important to know whom you're trading with (or against) because different market participants behave and trade in different ways. Understanding their strategies and goals can help you get a better outcome for your trade.

Brokers and dealers

Brokers and dealers are important characters when investing via dark pools; they're the ones who route your order and very often make the decision as to which dark pools to use. They can be individuals, small companies or subsidiaries of big banks who either trade for their own book (taking on risk and inventory themselves) or who execute orders on behalf of clients (that could be you). There is a slight distinction between a broker and a dealer. A *broker* is someone whose job it is to trade on behalf of others, whereas a *dealer* is someone who can also trade for his own account.

What distinguishes brokers and dealers from traders is that they're always professionals. On the other hand, *trader* describes either a professional or amateur who invests with a short-term horizon. This means he's trying to get in and out of a trade quickly. Unlike investors, traders seldom hold shares for long periods of time. Brokers and dealers don't always trade for their own book; they can charge a commission to execute a trade and earn that way. But traders always trade for their own book and make (or lose) their money solely on their trading in and out of stocks.

Brokers and dealers are part of the sell-side, because they're often trying to sell you something. (Other groups that make up the sell-side are research analysts, advisory firms and investment banking services, although investment bankers seldom operate in dark pools.) Brokers and dealers deal with both institutions and private individuals. They employ armies of analysts to research stocks and come up with buy, sell and hold recommendations and other investment ideas so that they can get their clients to take action and earn a commission for themselves in the process. The brokers and dealers execute or work the orders of their clients. They play an integral part in dark pools as they try to execute their clients' orders at the best possible prices.

Due to the sales-orientated business model, brokers and dealers, like market makers, add liquidity to the market by getting people and institutions to buy or sell stocks. They compete with other brokers and dealers in the market by promising clients better and faster execution of trades. Utilising dark pools is part of their sales pitch, because doing so allows them to promise clients a better quality of service and a guarantee of filling the clients' orders. Some brokers and dealers have in fact gone so far as to set up their own dark pools. For more information on broker-owned dark pools, refer to Chapter 4.

Private investors

Private investors are the people who buy and sell their personal holdings. If you have a portfolio of stocks and are buying or selling any of your holdings, you're involved as a private investor. You don't have to be a big-time institutional investor to participate in dark pool investing. When you make an order to buy or sell, you may have thought that it went straight to the stock market. Sometimes it does, and sometimes it doesn't. Your broker possibly routed your order instead to a dark pool.

Your broker may have done so for different reasons, but the primary consideration is money. For instance, your broker may also have a client who wants to sell the very stock you want to buy. What better way than to match the trade internally (known as *internalisation*)? That way the broker doesn't have to pay any fees to the stock exchange for the trade and he can pocket your full commission. In many places a client has to be asked if the trade can be matched internally, so if you're not new to this game, now you know why you might have heard the question.

Also, a dark pool may be cheaper than a stock market, so your broker decides to route your trade first through a dark pool to see whether the order can be matched there, saving the broker a penny or two in the process.

If you're giving a limit order to your broker then it's possible that he will pool your order with other orders at the same price and then place it in a dark pool. You may be a bit disconcerted if you have a live stock market feed and you sit there waiting for the order to come up on the screen. You may then call your broker and ask what's taking him so long to place the order. Your broker says that the order is placed. You say, 'Oh, no it's not.' And he answers, 'Oh, yes it is!' This pantomime can last all day or until your broker tells you that the trade is filled, leaving you scratching your head and thinking, 'What just happened?'

Rest assured, if your broker tells you that he placed your order, and you can't see it on a live stock market feed, then he has just routed it through a dark pool.

Regulators

Regulators have always been interested and involved in all trading markets. Dark pools are no different. Regulators advise, make rulings and police the markets. Decisions and actions made by them can alter the way markets operate. As an investor, you can't afford not to know what regulators are doing in regards to dark pools.

Regulators crave two things:

- ✔ **Control:** Regulators aim to control markets according to rules set up by them and legislators. Regulators also police markets and enforce the rules with the powers given to them by legislators. The main goal of the control is to provide an orderly and fair market to all participants.

- ✔ **Transparency:** Transparency is key to fair markets. If all participants can see what is going on in the market then it decreases opportunities for conduct that may be unfair to other market participants. Because dark pools by their nature aren't very transparent, they're facing an increasing amount of interest from regulators whose job it is to police the market.

Dark pools are a relatively new phenomena in the finance world, and high frequency trading (HFT) is an even newer phenomenon, so there isn't that much in the way of regulation at the moment. No one wants to see a repeat of the global financial meltdown, so increased regulation is something that the dark pools and high frequency traders are taking a keen interest in. Find out more about the changing world of dark pool regulation in Chapter 6.

You can be sure that in the upcoming years new regulations and big changes will occur in the market. These regulations and changes will have an effect on trading strategies and how the different market participants use dark pools. Two of the most powerful regulators regarding dark pools are as follows.

Securities and Exchanges Commission

The Securities and Exchanges Commission (SEC) oversees and regulates trading in the United States. Because the United States is the biggest and most powerful equities market in the world, the SEC is the most important force that determines the rules and direction of regulation concerning dark pools.

The SEC decides what the market participants have to follow. Make sure that you keep up to date and follow the commentary of the SEC to be aware of what possible changes are on the way that could affect the way dark pools operate.

The European Union

The member states that make up the European Union are important players in the dark pools arena. Just like in the United States, the Europeans have a keen interest in how equities are traded. With nearly 10 per cent of trades in

Europe being done through dark pools, regulators on the EU level are looking into dark pools and how they trade. The EU wants a transparent playing field and has therefore started to incorporate dark pools into the legislation it produces.

In Europe the main piece of legislation regarding how financial markets work is called the Markets in Financial Instruments Directive (MiFID). The European Union is now working on MiFID II. Preliminary reports already show that it's discussing dark pools and how it can bring more transparency into the market place to protect investors. Just like with the SEC, investors need to be aware of what is being discussed on an EU level because the EU and the United States both work together on financial market regulations.

Data centres

Data centres supply the computer hardware that provides the plumbing to make the market work. These providers are also the companies that make HFT possible.

In a market where trade execution is calculated in milliseconds, the data centres provide the infrastructure, the machines and a place where high frequency traders can house the powerful computers that execute their trading programs and algorithms guaranteeing fast execution of trades.

The data centres have been at the forefront of an arms race in which they compete for the business of high frequency traders by promising the most powerful and fastest service. It has reached the point where data centres are placed as close as possible to the venues where the trades are executed. This is known as *co-location*. By placing their servers close to the dark pools and stock exchanges precious milliseconds can be gained because the information flow has a shorter distance to travel.

Without superfast information and data flow the dark pools and high frequency traders can't execute their trades at the pace they need to be successful.

Journalists, bloggers and writers

Due to the relatively new phenomenon of dark pools and HFT and the lack of transparency and information regarding their activities they have captured the interest of the media, including all types of journalists, and even bloggers and other writers.

An increasing amount is being written about dark pools. The debate rages on in newspaper articles and blog posts, and new books are also coming out. This ongoing conversation is public, and many of these writers are being sought out as authorities on the market and their insight is being utilised by all participants. Both regulators and dark pool providers are using the opinions of journalists and other assorted pundits to improve and make changes to how they use dark pools.

Academia

Academics are playing an increasingly important role in the field of dark pools and HFT. All market participants, from traders and brokers and dealers to institutional investors, are using these findings to hone their trading strategies, and regulators are using the findings to identify areas where they can pinpoint inconsistencies and unfair practices.

An increasing number of academics have been researching the activities of dark pools and HFT and studying the effects of dark pools on financial markets, and a steady stream of papers is coming out on the subject. Some of these research papers go into minute details, breaking down trading and order flow data into millisecond increments.

As the debate surrounding dark pools and HFT gathers pace and interest in their activities grows among market participants, regulators and the general public, the kind of rigorous studies done by academics is important in shining a light on how dark pools operate.

Automated traders

Automated trading is the trading of equities using computer traded programs and algorithms. Instead of having a person sitting behind a trading terminal making the trading decisions and punching in orders on a computer, in automated trading a pre-programmed algorithm automatically makes decisions as to when to buy/sell, how much and at what price.

Some journalists and even some financial professionals incorrectly refer to automated trading as HFT. All HFT is automated, but not all automated trading is HFT. You can find out more about the practice of automated trading and HFT in Part III. These sections take a closer look at two types of automated trading and how they differ from each other.

Institutional automated traders

Institutions were one of the first to take up automated trading programs. Thanks to high frequency traders (more about them in the next section), lot sizes and the overall dollar amount of trades has decreased throughout the years, which has made executing orders challenging for large institutions. Institutions trade in very large amounts, often calculated in the millions and even tens of millions of dollars. Institutions are wary of moving the price adversely when executing a trade and therefore have developed special programs that try to limit the market impact of their orders.

When an institution makes a decision to buy or sell an equity, it can place that order using an automated trading program that drip-feeds the order to stock markets and various dark pools according to its own set criteria. This is why dark pools are such a favourite for institutional investors, because they can place an order into the market without having to reveal the overall size of the order.

High frequency traders

HFT is a big and important part of automated trading, but it's a unique and specific type of automated trading that sends out and cancels large amounts of small lot orders. It also tries to make tiny profits from quickly entering and exiting a trade and repeating this process as quickly and as often as possible.

Trading by high frequency traders makes up a large part of trading volume on the markets today. Though difficult to accurately gauge, it's estimated that in the United States it makes up more than 50 per cent of trades executed. In Europe the number is estimated to be 30 to 40 per cent and rising.

Utilising strategies

High frequency traders employ a multitude of different strategies, most of them based on making small profits by trading within the spread. Many of the strategies they employ are similar to traditional market makers. High frequency traders zip in and out of trades, making a few cents in the process and then repeating over and over again thousands of times. It all begins to add up to serious moolah. Refer to Chapter 12 for more information about some of these strategies.

Getting up to speed

When I talk about HFT, I refer to warp speed, Captain Kirk. From order to execution by a high frequency trader takes just a few milliseconds. To give you some idea of the kind of speed, it takes about 400 milliseconds for you to blink your eyes. There are literally things happening on the trading screen right before your eyes, but they're happening so quickly you can't see them.

One thing is a constant in HFT: the decisions are made and entered into by a computer program. High frequency traders use complex algorithms to execute their trading strategies. The algorithms analyse and make investment decisions, based on news flow affecting the markets and what is happening in the order book.

Considering dark pool rules

Other factors are exchange and dark pool rules. High frequency traders make use of dark pools as they execute trades in different markets and utilise the National Best Bid Offer (NBBO) in the lit markets and play within the spread. So in addition to speed, high frequency traders need market information. They often gather information by sending out small orders to try to determine whether there are big buyers or sellers in the market for any given stock. As a result of HFT, in recent years the average size of the bid and offer has decreased. The average dollar size of an executed trade today is just a few thousand dollars (previously the average trade used to be calculated in the tens of thousands of dollars) and the average lot size is now just a few hundred shares. This practice of sending out small orders is called *pinging*. Refer to Chapter 12 for more information.

Chapter 6

Regulating Dark Pools

· ·

In This Chapter

▶ Focusing on the importance of regulation

▶ Comprehending the impact of regulation in the United States and Europe

▶ Familiarising yourself with the major regulatory players

· ·

*T*he world of dark pools and high frequency trading (HFT) has come under the spotlight of regulators and legislators in recent years. (*Legislators* are the ones who create the laws that govern how the markets operate, whereas *regulators* are the organisations whose responsibility it is to monitor and enforce the rules made by the legislators.) This trend will only continue. In fact, the single biggest factor affecting the market is regulation. Without a doubt, dark pools and HFT will face more regulation, and certain market participants will try to find ways of getting around the new legislation or using it to gain an advantage.

When you have such a wide world of possibilities, problems can and do arise, all related to price. How can you be sure that you get the best possible price? What if the stock you want to buy is trading at a better price in another venue, but you don't have access to the venue with the better price? It's a bit like the question, 'If a tree falls in a forest and there's no one to see it, did it really happen?' Well, according to regulators, it most certainly did happen, and it's their job to try to shine a light on dark pools and make them a fair market to trade in for all participants.

The dark pool universe is constantly changing, so having a good understanding of the basic legislation that affects the world of dark pools and also being aware of the possible changes is vital. As technological innovations come into the market, legislators will be playing a game of catch-up.

 Legislation is the root of all major issues regarding dark pools and HFT. Legislation and how it affects you as an investor differ based on jurisdiction. But don't worry; you don't need to know the ins and outs of each and every law across the world concerning dark pools and HFT. This chapter provides a basic framework of how dark pools and HFT operate in the market in which you're trading. In addition, I take a closer look at US legislation and the European Union (EU) legislation and how they are affected by each other. Those markets are the largest and also serve as trendsetters in dark pools and HFT for the rest of the world. Other emerging markets looking to expand into dark pools are keen to attract HFT traders because doing so fills up order books in their illiquid markets, bringing about the appearance of liquidity and tighter spreads for investors.

Relating to Regulation

Dark pools and HFT markets came into being because of legislative loopholes. As a result, any changes in the regulation and oversight of the market will have far-reaching and immediate effects. Legislation moves slowly in the planning stage where discussion and debate happen. Thanks to the way information is handled nowadays, most of that debate is public. By having a sound understanding of the legislative foundation of dark pools and following the debate about suggested changes and tweaks to the rules, you can tune your own trading so as not to be adversely affected by any changes. Who knows, perhaps you'll even be able to take advantage of any possible legislative changes.

The following sections explain exactly what regulation is, why you need to be aware of legislation and regulation, and what you can do to be more aware.

Defining regulation and legislation

Regulation of markets and dark pools is generally carried out by specific organisations set up for the task of enforcing and guiding financial markets. Usually, this entity in a country is tasked with the overseeing of financial markets, although some countries (such as the United States) may have several regulatory bodies overseeing different sectors of the financial markets.

The enforcement powers are given to regulators by *legislation*, which is made up of the laws that govern financial markets. These laws are national; however, a drive in the EU has called for common, unified legislation.

Regulation and the legislation that backs it aim to provide and support a fair market and also create a framework to extract taxes. When concerning regulation, legislation comes down to two areas:

✔ **Fairness:** People interpret fairness differently depending on what side of the issues they're viewing it from. *Fairness* basically means a market level and transparent for all participants – from the small private investor to the large institutional behemoth. The concept of a fair market is the major driver in legislation. Often the results that come from legislation can be unexpected and unseen, but nonetheless it's the concept of fairness that's used as justification for legislation.

✔ **Money:** When it comes to legislation, money tends to be synonymous with taxes. Whenever there's any form of business transaction governments inevitably start to think that perhaps they can tax it. For governments the vast amount of money that sloshes about in the markets and that is touched by HFT and dark pools is a temptation hard to pass up.

In other words, the aim of changes in legislation to dark pools and HFT usually focuses on creating a fair and even playing field for all market participants. Achieving this aim is by no means an easy task and often results with a bit of a belly-flop – and eventually takes a cut for the government via some form of tax.

Taking action to be more empowered about legislation and regulation

Currently, the debate and discussion around dark pools is global and the hottest subject in the financial sector. With so much interest, new legislation and new rules are forthcoming, and the effects they'll have on the market are unknown. Although designed to do one thing, they may well end up having completely unexpected results. That's why keeping constantly updated on any changes is important.

Pay close attention to any discussions relating to possible new legislation planned for dark pools and HFT. When new laws and rules are implemented, they will affect how your trades are processed and executed. If you aren't up to date on the changes and how they relate to your investing practices then you could end up paying for it.

You don't need to read each piece of proposed legislation that comes out. Doing so would be an exercise in futility and a test of your threshold for boredom. Because a small change in legislation can bring about big changes in the market, you do need to know what's going on. You need to see the big picture. The easiest way to do this is to set up some Google News alerts with the key words 'MiFID', 'Reg NMS' and 'Financial Transaction Tax'. In this way, when things do move on the legislative front, you should receive timely information from an assortment of reliable sources straight to your email account.

If you want to delve deeper into the effects of current legislation, search out academic research on how legislation has affected electronic trading. To get the best outcome, first read the abstract of the study and then read the conclusions and have a look at the sources for further interesting reading. After doing so, feel free to read the whole paper. In this way you gain an overall understanding of the findings of researchers and find other related research without spending time reading things that may be irrelevant.

Eyeing Regulation of Dark Pools in the United States: Reg NMS

Dark pools started in the United States, the country of free enterprise. People tend to have a common vision of American stock markets as places where fellows in colourful jackets walk around the floor of the New York Stock Exchange waving at each other. Although that picture may have been true at one time, it's no longer true. Today trading happens via computers and that trading happens on multiple platforms. Several markets exist, not just one single stock exchange, and these markets are lit and dark, all competing for order flow. You can now trade in one single stock in an assortment of trading venues – simultaneously. The idea is that in a fair market the best possible price at the moment should be available to all participants.

With so many different types of trading venues, legislators in the United States have tried (and continue to try) to come up with legislation that makes the markets an even playing field for all participants – from mom-and-pop investors to HFT firms and everyone in between. That's where Regulation National Market System (Reg NMS for short) comes into play. It's at the root of all legislation relating to dark pools and HFT in the United States. In fact, Reg NMS gave birth to HFT.

Reg NMS came into force in 2007; it's a set of rules compiled by the US Securities and Exchange Commission (SEC) that defines how individual trading venues operate within the market as a whole. The idea was simple enough: to set guidelines for an efficient market, the integrity of which all market participants can rely upon.

The United States had, and still has, a large number of market venues. When Reg NMS came into force, it brought three specific things with it that shaped today's market. They are as follows (the following sections discuss each in greater depth):

- Rule 610: The market access rule
- Rule 611: The order protection rule
- Rule 612: The sub-penny rule

Although you don't have to study the 500 pages of legalise that make up Reg NMS, you do need to understand the framework as well as a few of the critical points within the legislation that are vital in the running of the market. You also need to know some of the points of contention surrounding Reg NMS. When you get a group of finance geeks together and they start discussing Reg NMS, you see sparks flying. A few points in Reg NMS cause a lot of debate, particularly the National Best Bid Offer (NBBO) and the rule on locked markets. The basic concept is easy: all exchanges and market venues send their bids and offers to the Security Information Processor (SIP). The best bid and the best offer then make up the NBBO, both of which are protected.

Rule 610: The market access rule

Rule 611 on order protection (check out the next section for more on this rule) provides the best possible price to all market participants, but you can't provide the best possible price unless you give access to all market venues to all participants. That's where rule 610 comes into play. The most important thing to keep in mind regarding rule 610, the market access rule, often called the *rule on locked markets*, is its ban on locked and crossed markets.

A market is *locked* when a bid and an offer of equal price occur in two separate market venues. For example, Market A has a bid of $10 and Market B has an offer of $10. The market is now locked. In an efficient and properly working market, these two trades should be matched with each other and the trade executed, nothing else. Meanwhile, a *crossed* market is one in which the spread between bid and offer is negative. Put another way, the offer is lower than the bid.

Having a locked market shows an inefficient market and causes all-round confusion and a general air of befuddlement among traders. A locked market doesn't make for an orderly market, and it certainly doesn't guarantee best execution because market participants can't be confident that they're getting the best price at that particular time. The SEC puts it this way: 'Locks and crosses are inconsistent with fair and orderly markets and detract from market efficiency.'

A crossed market is even worse; the bid is higher than the offer in another market, which means that both the buyer and the seller aren't getting the best execution possible. The buyer is willing to pay more than the price at which the seller is willing to sell the shares. In an orderly market this shouldn't happen.

The other main issue that rule 610 deals with is fees. Each venue has its own fee structure and entry requirements regarding membership. By allowing access to outside participants, there is the danger that those participants who aren't members of a particular venue incur extra costs for getting their orders executed. Rule 610 sets limits on fees and attempts to create a level playing field for all.

Rule 611: The order protection rule

The aim of the *order protection rule* is to give all investors the best possible price at the time of their trade. It states that if an order coming into a market can be traded at a better price in another market venue then that order must be directed to and executed in the venue with the best price.

This rule, sometimes referred to as the *trade-through rule*, stops orders being traded through. An order is *traded through* if a better price could have been obtained at the same time in another exchange venue. To implement this rule, all trading centres are required to maintain and enforce procedures that prevent trade-through trades from happening.

This rule is designed to encourage limit orders. Without an abundance of limit orders there wouldn't be a market. Everyone would just be sitting around wondering what the stock would be worth, not knowing whether there were any buyers or sellers out there. Encouraging market participants to place limit orders gets what is known as price discovery. *Price discovery* is simply the process of buy and sell orders coming into the market and letting the supply and demand determine the price of the stock. The process of price discovery shows you exactly where the market currently values an individual stock. Limit orders also increase liquidity, and buyers and sellers can confidently trade by being able to see how much of a stock is on offer and at what price.

As for dark pools, they take their price from the NBBO, which is supplied by the Securities Information Processor (SIP). This is a consolidated feed of all the limit orders in the various US stock exchanges. These limit orders act as a benchmark for the trades executed in dark pools. The best bid and the best offer of the SIP feed make up the NBBO. Both the best bid and the best offer are *protected*, meaning that they have priority of execution regardless of what exchange you're trading on. This guarantees that market participants always get the best possible available price.

A *protected quote* must be the best bid or best offer on one of the national securities exchanges sent to the SIP, and it must also be immediately executable and automated. It isn't just a limit order. It must be doable with a click of a button. It must also be executable as an immediate or cancel (IOC) order, which means that if any part of an incoming order can't be filled at that price then it's automatically cancelled and not routed to another market, *unless* the participant submitting the order instructs to route any unfilled part of the order to another exchange. (Refer to Chapter 8 for more on the ins and outs of an IOC order.)

For example, if the National Association of Securities Dealers Automated Quotation (NASDAQ) has the best bid for a stock at $20 but has no matching offer, but the New York Stock Exchange (NYSE) gets an order to sell the same stock at $20, the NYSE would be obligated to route that order to the NASDAQ where it would be executed. (The NASDAQ order was the best bid and thus protected.)

The order protection rule does have an important exception: the inter-market sweep order (ISO). These orders aren't for retail investors; they're for the big boys packing big heat. In all its simplicity it works like this:

Say you want to buy 1,000 shares of stock Alpha at $5.01. You see that there are 200 shares offered at exactly $5. Now, going by the strict letter of Reg NMS you would get the 200 shares at $5 and then you'd have to place another order for the remaining 800 shares at $5.01. With an ISO order what happens is that you get your 200 shares at $5 and then the remainder of your order is re-routed to other venues to try to pick up the remainder of the shares. Check out Chapter 9 for more information on ISOs.

Rule 612: The sub-penny rule

The *sub-penny rule* states that no stock can be traded in increments below $0.01. Remember, the US markets only changed from fractions to decimals in their trading in 2001. The result was that spreads decreased, and all was well with the world and investors were happy.

Having sub-penny increments is forbidden for a couple of reasons:

✔ These small increments reduce the depth of the market. Imagine having an order book in which the top bids were $10.004, $10.003, $10.002, $10.001 and so on. Such prices don't really give you information regarding the proper price, so sub-penny increments can be seen as detrimental to the concept of price discovery.

✔ Traders (particularly HFT traders) can easily jump in front of a limit order with sub-penny differences in price. Rule 612 addresses this issue. It states that no exchange, market venue, or broker or dealer can accept an order or an indication of interest quoted at less than a penny.

But as always, there's an exception. That is for stocks priced below a dollar. These stocks are commonly referred to as *penny stocks*, and they can be denominated in sub-penny increments.

Looking at Europe — the Fastest-Growing Dark Pool Fixture

Currently, HFT trading represents about 30 to 40 per cent of trading in the European markets, so it's no surprise that the European Union (EU) wants to legislate it more. In Europe, the drive has been to legislate markets so that all EU member states have the same legislation.

Despite working together for financial reform, European countries still have their own national legislation. For instance, Germany has been the first to implement a law dealing with HFT companies that requires them to register and report their trading strategies to national authorities. Italy and France have placed taxes on financial transactions. Any form of trade taxation understandably affects HFT firms, which turn over a massive amount of stocks.

Although these differences in laws exist, the EU, as a whole, has enacted some common legislation to regulate dark pools and HFT. The following sections examine the legislation and point out just what you need to know. Know that all the EU members strive to have uniform legislation regarding their financial markets. They do so by enacting EU-wide directives that member states must incorporate into their own legislation.

Markets in Financial Instruments Directive

The Markets in Financial Instruments Directive, or MiFID as it is more commonly known, is the bible of all European financial services businesses. All member states are obligated to implement the rules and procedures set out in MiFID. Think of MiFID as the minimum standard that all EU member states must follow. MiFID is a bit scary and vengeful, and no one in the business dares to mess with it. The law is rather long and not very exciting reading.

MiFID has two parts:

- MiFID I, which is the original
- MiFID II, which the EU is currently working on to build on MiFID I

I won't bore you with all the details of the law. The next sections give an overview of these two sections of the law.

MiFID I

MiFID I was drafted in 2004 and came into force in 2007. These dates are significant in that HFT and dark pools' growth came about after 2007. Because the legislation was written as early as 2004, very little in MiFID is aimed at HFT and dark pools directly, simply for the reason that EU legislators knew nothing about them; they didn't even know that such beasts existed. MiFID I focuses on the general principle of open and transparent markets, such as pre- and post-trade reporting standards and investor protection.

MiFID has had amendments after 2007, most notably in 2008 and 2010, but these amendments didn't relate directly to HFT or dark pools.

MiFID II

Where MiFID I is vague on HFT and dark pools, MiFID II is aimed directly at the HFT and dark pool universe. If you're trading using any form of algorithm then MiFID II is gunning for you. So what can you expect?

In the proposed MiFID II, a section deals specifically with algorithmic trading. Unsurprisingly, it's called Article 17 Algorithmic Trading. It contains these important proposals for firms operating algorithmic trading models:

- ✔ Trading firms using algorithmic trading models must ensure that their trading models are resilient regardless of market conditions.

- ✔ Firms must provide details of their trading models to their national financial oversight authority.

- ✔ Firms must keep records of their trading and their algorithmic models and make them available to the authorities upon request.

- ✔ Algorithmic models must be in continuous operation during the trading day, regardless of market conditions, thus providing liquidity to the market.

These suggestions do pose a very real threat to HFT firms because many will feel that revealing their trading strategies could affect their returns.

There is one proposal that appears to have been excluded, one that would have killed off HFT totally. In negotiations this proposal was referred to as the *minimum resting period*. The original suggestion by legislators was to implement a minimum holding period for orders of 500 milliseconds. Because it is exactly below this time that HFT operates, such a proposal would have meant the end of HFT in Europe. Legislators were clearly too scared of the possible impact to spreads and liquidity if more than 30 to 40 per cent of the value of trading within the European markets suddenly disappeared.

Financial transaction tax (FTT)

A *financial transaction tax* (FTT) is a tax placed on executed trades, changed orders or cancelled orders. The result would be that governments gain tax revenue while decreasing excessive HFT trading (however that may be defined). Those opposed to the tax argue that it would take away liquidity from markets and increase the bid-offer spread, thus increasing costs to end investors. There is also the argument that any FTT designed specifically to target HFT and dark pools would be discriminatory and would place some investors on an unequal footing to others.

MiFID doesn't include a FTT, but the FTT discussion is closely linked with any discussion regarding MiFID. Although MiFID II is a coming inevitability in one form or another, a European FTT isn't a sure thing.

However, the concept of a FTT has popular appeal in some European countries, and about a dozen countries are keen to implement the tax in one form or another. The general consensus is that FTT should be equal across all European markets. This hasn't stopped some countries implementing one unilaterally, though.

France placed a FTT on its stock exchange in 2012, and despite warnings of impending doom and the end of the stock market in France by those opposed to the tax, trading didn't come to an end in Paris. Understandably, though, liquidity did decrease and spreads widened somewhat.

Italy implemented its own FTT in 2012 specifically to target HFTs. The tax of 0.02 per cent is placed on all order changes and cancellations placed within a 0.5 second time-frame.

Germany has not implemented a FTT but it has implemented a law regarding HFTs.

Because the big countries of the EU – France, Italy and Germany – are legislating HFTs already, it's possible that eventually a Europe-wide FTT will be put into place.

Considering Other Markets

The United States and Europe are still the biggest markets for dark pools, but you shouldn't forget the other major markets in the world, particularly Asia, which is growing rapidly. These markets take their lead from the main markets of the United States and Europe, so the similarities in rules governing dark pools are strong, but if you invest globally, it's good to know some of the basic regulatory issues of the other main global markets.

Canada

Canada's dark pool market is relatively small when compared to the major markets, but regulators haven't been inactive when it comes to dark pools. In 2012 the Investment Industry Regulatory Organisation of Canada (IIROC) placed new rules on dark pools and how orders between the displayed markets and dark pools would be transacted.

The rules stipulated that when there was an equal order in a dark pool and a displayed stock exchange, the stock exchange order would have priority. Also, only trades that proved price improvement would be allowed to be executed in a dark pool. The rules caused criticism from Canadian dark pool providers that trading would migrate across the border to the United States and result in a loss of liquidity.

Asia

Trading on dark pools in Asia remains small, with the vast majority of trades still executed in the displayed stock exchanges. The main markets in Asia are Japan, Hong Kong and Singapore. The regulatory landscape in these markets closely follows those of the also may have an influence on regulators in these markets.

The Asian markets are looking for growth, which means attracting further liquidity. Doing so often involves courting automated traders, which is a fine balancing act for the Asian regulators, who are closely observing the dark pool market but have remained relatively silent on any major changes. The only one that has come out with anything significant is the Hong Kong Securities and Futures Commission, which has stated that it may look at banning retail investors from dark pools; however, nothing has been implemented.

Australia

You wouldn't think Australia was forerunner in the dark pool market, but in 2013 the Australian Securities and Investments Commission (ASIC) implemented changes to the way dark pools were operated in Australia, which could be something that other jurisdictions take up.

ASIC had discovered that the size of individual trades executed on dark pools had declined. Dark pools were originally designed to match large block orders, so ASIC wanted to push these smaller trades back into the displayed market where it felt the orders really belonged. ASIC implemented a rule that if an order wasn't a block trade then the order had to prove that it could offer price improvement to what was offered in the displayed market. If not then it would have to be executed on the displayed market. What qualifies as a block trade is dependent on the average volume of the stock in question.

This small adjustment seems to have worked because the volume of smaller trades has decreased in the dark pools and increased in the displayed markets.

Part III
Coming to Grips with Automated Trading

Top five ways to begin your battle against the algorithms

- **Explore what an algorithm does.** Algorithms are all over the place in the investing world; they're present in dark pools and displayed markets. If you know what they do, you'll be better able to spot them.

- **Discover the importance of price time priority.** Figure out the principle that all markets have operated by and how it has been jeopardised by high frequency trading.

- **Identify the different order types.** Knowing the different order types used against you by high frequency traders makes you a savvier investor.

- **Understand the need for speed.** High frequency trading is about speed. Most investors won't have the same access to speed as high frequency traders, but the playing field is levelling out.

- **Practise spotting high frequency traders in action.** Investing in today's markets is about making sure you aren't the prey. Spotting the high frequency traders in action helps you with your investing.

 Get more information on high frequency trading strategies and how they operate on the markets by visiting www.dummies.com/extras/darkpools.

In this part . . .

✔ Find out all about quantitative analysts and how they changed the market by building algorithmic trading models.

✔ Explore the standard order types and also the special order types that haven't been publicly discussed and that exchanges and high frequency traders have kept hidden.

✔ Discover why co-location and speed are important parts of high frequency trading and how they affect trading.

✔ Spot the different types of high frequency trading strategies used in the markets and identify the ways algorithms can be used to game the markets.

Chapter 7

Comprehending Automated Trading

In This Chapter

▶ Knowing who creates automated trading systems

▶ Running an automated trading strategy

▶ Examining the importance of algorithms

*A*utomated computer programmed trading is a major function in dark pools (as well as in lit markets). It provides much of the liquidity and market depth in today's markets. Often thought to be the same as high frequency trading (HFT), automated trading is in fact quite different. Although all HFT is automated trading, not all automated trading is HFT, as this chapter explains.

Automated trading is a major part of today's financial markets. In one form or another, nearly all professional market participants use it. Traditional market makers, traders and institutions mainly use automated trading to execute large orders. To fully comprehend how the markets work, you need to have a basic knowledge of automated trading and algorithms. You don't need to become a quantitative analyst yourself or build your own algorithms. As technology progresses you'll find more automated trading processes being offered to you. By knowing how they work, you'll be better equipped to get the most out of these tools for your own trading.

Most of the new regulations affecting the markets relate to market microstructure, which includes automated trading. You need to know the basics of automated trading to grasp how changes in market rules will affect your trading.

When buying or selling stocks, your order will often be executed against an automated trading program. Understanding the effect that your orders can have on automated programs is important to enable you to get the best possible price for yourself. Also, recognising when a special order type has been on the other end of your trade can help you use strategies to mitigate their impact on your price.

Identifying Quantitative Analysts

Quantitative analysts are the people who are responsible for building, running and testing automated trading systems. When you invest in the markets these days, particularly if you or your broker is doing it via a dark pool, you'll be coming up against quantitative models and the quantitative analysts who built them. Knowing who these analysts are and how they operate is important for you.

These sections take a closer look at what characteristics are important for quantitative analysts and what, specifically, they do.

Because the word *quantitative* is a bit of a mouthful and rather difficult to spell, quantitative analysts are commonly referred to just as *quants*.

What makes a good quant

Quants are particularly good at maths, which is exactly what their job entails. Their job is to analyse financial data, build mathematical models based on that data, put it all into a computer program and turn that baby on, bringing in plenty of money for their firm. Well, that's the idea at least. It sounds simple, but it's not.

Quants are highly educated and capable at what they do. They come mainly from a mathematics, engineering or physics background. Many have a long career behind them in academia and they often hold PhDs. When it comes to numbers, these people know their stuff.

Being a whiz at numbers isn't enough, though. A quant also needs the ability to put those numbers to work, and nowadays, as everyone knows, numbers are put to work using a computer. Therefore, in addition to mathematical modelling skills, quants need computer programming skills.

Quants were originally specialists in pricing complex derivatives. *Derivatives* are investments whose value is derived (there's the clue) from another underlying asset. Nowadays quants are involved in more than just derivatives. Their skills are now used in most fields of finance, including risk management, portfolio modelling and trading strategies, particularly HFT strategies.

A brief snapshot of the history of quants

Quantitative analysis has been around for some time, but it really started to grow as a career in the late nineties and blossomed into the limelight with the rise of hedge funds in the early millennium.

In 1990 hedge funds held an average of $39 billion in assets under management. Within a decade it had grown to $490 billion. Before the beginning of the global financial crisis in 2007 hedge funds held assets in excess of $2 trillion, all fuelled by massive leverage and presided over by an army of quants who devised the various and myriad investment strategies of the hedge funds.

As the industry ballooned, it started to have its own superstars. Many quants became celebrities in their own right, becoming heroes to investors with their faces on the covers of *Forbes* and *Fortune*.

When the quants get it right, they get it right in a big way. One of the most famous quants is Jim Simons, who runs the Renaissance Medallion fund. This hedge fund has returned an average of 40 per cent per year for more than two decades. It has made Simons a legend in the investment community and one of the wealthiest men in the world. As a comparison, the historical average return of the stock market has been around 8 per cent.

Renaissance Medallion is a good example of a quant-driven fund. Of its 200 employees a third has PhDs in non-finance subjects like maths, physics and engineering.

Success has a way of bringing about enemies, which is no different for quants. Some, mainly traditional traders who tend not to have much love for the modern quant, dislike them. This may well be due to the fact that quants tend to be academic and bookish, whereas traditional traders are known for being rather brash and outspoken.

Some academics, politicians and media pundits argue that quants have a negative effect on other industries because the financial industry hires so much top talent — talent that could be used in pursuit of other scientific endeavours. Lured into the world of finance by the potential rich rewards, industries like medical research, for example, lose out on some of the best talent.

Whether a good thing or a bad thing, the fact is that quants are very much part of the financial markets and they're major influencers in that sector. If you trade any financial instrument, you'll be working with or up against quants.

What quants do

Grasping what quants do is good way for you to understand the process that an automated trading program goes through from an initial idea to an actual real, working program that sends and executes orders in the market.

Building a proper, working, automated trading program requires four essential elements:

✔ Data (lots of it)

✔ Analysis

✔ Testing

✔ Live trading

These sections explain the elements in depth to help you grasp what quants do in their day-to-day jobs. If you find yourself wanting to have a go at actually building a real trading algorithm then you should read *Algorithmic Trading: Winning Strategies and Their Rationale* by Ernie Chan (John Wiley & Sons, Inc.).

Mining for data gold dust

To start the process a quant needs data – lots of data. Quants get their data from various vendors who supply very specific market data, such as Reuters and Bloomberg. You can gain access to market data vendors such as Bloomberg and Reuters if you have the money, but bear in mind their services are by no means cheap. A single Bloomberg terminal will set you back about $2,000 per month. Some brokers will allow access to their own database for their trading clients, but this is normally contingent on the client trading a certain amount of volume on a regular basis.

Depending on the strategy, a quant gathers market data on a chosen market from an appropriate time interval. For example, if the investment strategy is one in which a certain stock is traded within milliseconds on a high powered computer then the quant requires data of each trade done to the closest millisecond with information regarding the price, size of the trade and the executing trader (if possible). In such a strategy, news and fundamental analysis isn't necessary, just cold, hard trade data.

The very essence of quantitative analysis is the belief that with enough computer power and with the right trading strategy the market can be beaten. The amounts of data used can be staggering. HFT quants can download trade data including data such as price, volume, broker and time (down to the millisecond). With heavily traded stocks this can include millions of different variables per day. When going through data spanning several decades, it becomes obvious that the computing power needed to handle such amounts of information is vast.

Analysing the pieces

After a quant collects the data, he needs to analyse it all. The best way to do so is for the quant to enter the data into the platform that issued for the analysis. The quant can begin to work his magic. The most basic and still widely used platform for analysis is Microsoft Excel. In fact, Excel is so common that many commonly available advanced platforms are Excel-based, such as Reuters.

The quant performs various mathematical calculations, trying to discover patterns, however miniscule, that show something that no one has discovered before, something that will give an edge to the quant and a reveal a trading strategy that could be profitable.

Testing the engine

The analysed data is just theoretical, so the quant needs to test it on the market. When testing, a quant will first conduct a *back test*, which involves pitting the calculations against historical market data. This stage is a 'what if' kind of testing. It tells the quant whether the strategy used would have been historically profitable. There are, however, two problems with this testing:

- ✔ **Historical returns are never a guarantee of future returns.** Looking at the history is important, because much of what happens in the markets is cyclical and has a tendency to repeat itself. However, just because a trading strategy would have worked in the past doesn't mean that it will work now or in the future. Markets evolve and change, and historical back testing is unable to take account of these types of changes.

- ✔ **The orders were never really placed into the market.** This problem is bigger; no strategy can be tested without putting money down. Every single order placed in the market has an effect on the order book and the trading. Just because something works well on paper doesn't mean that when it's implemented in real life it won't have a completely different effect. After you're a participant in the game, you become part of it and your actions affect the actions of others and possibly change the outcomes.

Trading live

Trading live is the real test of the automated trading system – when it's plugged into the market and begins to send out real orders for real money. In the beginning stages, it's common to use smaller amounts of money so if something does go wrong or needs to be adjusted then the losses aren't too big.

Why quants are essential

Globalisation and computerisation were prerequisites to the rise of quantitative finance. Before that, trading and financial markets were a localised affair. Investment decisions and trading positions were taken based on rumours, opinions of industry peers and general newsflow. This is still the case, but now the amount of data being produced at a constant rate is too much for the human mind to handle. Even if humans could handle this amount of data, humans can't physically execute an order at the same speed a computer can.

As the world, including financial markets, has become more and more connected, computerised analysis and execution of investment decisions has become a necessity. This is the reason that quants have become so important. Their skills truly changed the market and have helped build a global network that works at a speed calculated in the milliseconds.

Humans are still needed for the planning of strategies, but the execution of the strategies requires the skills of the quants.

Entering the Realm of the Algorithm

The computerised algorithm has revolutionised financial markets and trading. Giving an exact amount of trading done via algorithms is difficult, but estimates for the US markets alone are in the region of 60 per cent of all trades.

With the constant speeding up of financial markets, the need for algorithms continues to grow. Humans continue to be responsible for setting the parameters and the rules for investing, but the timing and execution of trades is becoming ever more automated requiring the use of algorithms.

Eventually, retail investors will also be given access to forms of algorithmic trading platforms where they can themselves decide on the conditions of when a trade is entered into the market. These investors will then be able to let the algorithm execute that trade when the pre-set conditions are fulfilled in the market.

This section looks at the specifics you need to build an algorithm, from knowing exactly what an algorithm is and does to the different languages required and also the specific steps that you have to take to get to a working trading algorithm. If you want to dive into building an algorithm yourself, read *Quantitative Trading: How to Build Your Own Algorithmic Trading Business* by Ernie Chan (John Wiley & Sons, Inc.).

Knowing what an algorithm is

An algorithm is at the very heart of automated trading. There can be no automated trading without algorithms. With algorithmic trading, *algo trading* and *automated trading* are used as synonyms. In its simplest form, an *algorithm* is a formula that solves a particular question. It's a set of strict, step by step mathematical rules that end up giving you an answer to a mathematical problem.

If you've ever used Microsoft Excel, the chances are you've used an algorithm. Finding the largest number in a list of numbers is a simple form of an
algorithm. If you drill down to the very nitty gritty of an algorithm, you'll find
that it is just a string of *if–then* calculations, the length of which depends on
the complexity of the mathematical problem in question.

The great thing about algorithms is that when put into a computer, they can
calculate masses of data in a very fast time, exactly what is needed in a financial trading model.

Building an algorithm

Creating an algorithm isn't a difficult task; you simply need a basic understanding of Microsoft Excel. The problems arise when you have to calculate
masses of data from various different sources.

Algorithms for trading purposes are built using a multitude of computer languages. If you're versed in computer languages, you can choose the best possible language for your specific needs; if not then you'll need to do what most
of the financial world does and employ a quant or a computer programmer.

The most common languages for algorithmic programming are the following:

- ✔ C++
- ✔ Java
- ✔ Python
- ✔ Perl

These languages can be broken down into two types:

- ✔ **Statically:** These perform checks on the program during the compilation
  process. C++ and Java are examples.
- ✔ **Dynamically typed:** These perform the checks when the program is running. Python and Perl are examples.

The first thing to do when you're deciding on what language is best for your
trading program is to split the algorithm into five parts:

- ✔ Data
- ✔ Execution
- ✔ Portfolio management

- ✔ Hardware
- ✔ Latency

These sections take a closer look at these five parts and how you can go about collecting the necessary data and what steps you need to take to put it all together for a working algorithm.

Data

The *data* is the information that is evaluated and back tested, thus generating a trading signal. The amount of data analysed and the frequency of its use is a driving factor in the choice of computer language.

Various sources for data are available. You can find specialist firms that sell access to data like Bloomberg or Reuters. Sometimes your broker will be able to supply you with data, so be sure to discuss with him what he offers and also ask other providers what data options they can offer you. You also can access free sources of data, such as Yahoo Finance or Google Finance.

For example, if you're developing a trading strategy evolving around a single equity, it would require less data than a strategy trading the whole of the S&P 500 index.

Execution

The *execution* involves the signal generated by the trading program to initiate an order to the market. Matters such as network speed and reliability are important. You have to be confident that the program you use is reliable, and you need to be able to get in and out of a trade when you want. Reliability is paramount because an unreliable program can leave you holding stock that you wanted to sell or it can hinder you from getting a trade executed when you most need it.

Speed is also important because markets can move very quickly; the fact that your program has generated an order to buy or sell isn't enough. It needs to execute it quickly, because that opportunity to buy or sell maybe around for just a split second.

When you want to execute a trade with an automated program, the ability of outside parties such as brokers, exchanges and dark pools to communicate with your program becomes a critical issue. It's important that the algorithm speaks a language understood by the third parties and also does so reliably.

In an HFT strategy calculated in milliseconds, speed is uber important and therefore co-location becomes a criterion (see the later section 'Hardware' for more details on co-location). If the exchange doesn't offer co-location services and the strategy involves an HFT model then any advantage may be lost, whereas the execution order travels to the exchange or dark pool via a broker information leakage can occur slowing down the trade execution.

Portfolio management

An important criterion often overlooked is *portfolio management*, which involves managing the risk of the trading strategy. This part of the algorithm answers the question: what if? Portfolio management has to be automated and built in as part of your algorithm. It answers as many as possible of the questions related to the risks that can adversely affect your trading strategy.

Because market forces can be unpredictable, any strategy must have scenarios of what to do if something unexpected happens. The following are just some of the factors that will affect the portfolio management strategy:

- ✔ **News flow on the price of the underlying stock or related stocks:** News flow can have an effect on a stock's price, particularly if the news is a surprise to the market.

- ✔ **Volatility of the overall market:** Your stock isn't an island. Other factors happening in the market affect it, which is why your algorithms have to also take into account the movement of the overall market and how it correlates to your stock.

- ✔ **Counter-party default:** Stocks aren't settled immediately. Normally, settlement is a few days after the trade is executed, which means that there is a risk that the party you have traded with is unable to deliver or pay for the shares.

- ✔ **Server failures:** An algorithm acts with many other participants in the market. What happens if your computers or a third party you need to use, such as an exchange or dark pool, has a server failure? You need to have a plan for how such an event is handled by your automated trading program.

- ✔ **Program bugs:** You must have a working kill switch built into your algorithm. If your algorithm starts trading in an unintended manner, you need to be able to stop it quickly because a computer program bug can cause huge financial damage in a very short amount of time.

- ✔ **Black swan events:** Coined by the author and fund manager Nassim Taleb, a *black swan event* is a sudden market-impacting event that is unexpected and hasn't been taken into consideration by a trading model.

Hardware

When you're building your trading algorithm, you need to think about the hardware you require. Will a simple desktop machine suffice, or do you need a remote server or cloud provider? If you're operating an ultra-high frequency strategy, you might need a co-located server. It all comes down to reliability and speed.

Having a desktop machine can be great because it's simple and is in your office or home, but issues such as connectivity are a real risk. If you ever spill your coffee on your desktop then all your hard work will be lost. You know it can happen.

Remote- and cloud-based servers tend to be more reliable than desktop machines. You're also able to store more data there, but you need to log in to access them, which is a problem if you're prone to forgetting or losing passwords from time to time. They aren't completely free from technical issues. Pricewise they also have extra costs on top of a desktop option.

Co-located servers are in fact the same as remote servers; they're just located next to or very close to the exchange and give you lower latency. Co-located servers are absolutely essential if your strategy employs an HFT model.

Latency

Latency is the time it takes between an event trigger and a response. For trading purposes, it can be thought of as the time it takes for a trading signal (the *trigger*) to generate to execution of the trade (the *response*).

Think of latency as a form of delay from deciding you want to do something and then being able to see it through to its conclusion. The lower the latency, the quicker you can go from decision to a completed action.

 Things have a habit of going bump at the most inopportune moment; the biggest profits are often made in fast-moving markets that often involve large volumes. These volumes cause traffic and will therefore put a strain on your hardware and on your trading program. You must have a good quality system that works well and is resilient in times of stress.

Letting an algorithm loose on the markets

After planning and back testing your algorithm, it's time to put it into action in the real world. When discussing or reading about automated trading systems, the following terms will inevitably come up, which is why it's important that you know their main attributes.

The four types of algorithms that most program-based trading strategies can be placed in are as follows.

Volume-Weighted Average Price (VWAP)

This type of algorithm calculates the average price of a stock based on the volumes traded. A volume-weighted average price (VWAP) algorithm attempts to execute trades at a price close to or better than the market

VWAP. The VWAP is the benchmark of the execution. Because the VWAP is a simple calculation, VWAP strategies tend to be basic in nature.

Daily volumes for stocks are fairly regular in nature. In the United States, most of the trading is done in the morning and late afternoon with a lull at midday (traders and quants have to eat too, right?). When put in a graph, this trading produces a U-shape.

For example, you buy 900 shares of Acme, Inc.: 500 shares at $20, 300 shares at $20.50 and 100 shares at $21. Your VWAP for the share is as follows:

$$\frac{(500 \times 20) + (300 \times 20.5) + (100 \times 21)}{900} = \$20.28 \text{ VWAP}$$

In Europe the majority of trading is done in the afternoon (when the US markets are also open). On a graph, this type of trading that tends to be mostly carried out in the afternoon produces a rising slope shape.

For a VWAP strategy, decide how long the order will run for. It could be a few minutes or for the whole trading day. For the chosen timeframe, a volume profile is used (remember the U-shape or the rising slope profile!). The order is then placed in the market in small numbers based on a percentage of the volume profile.

VWAP strategies are popular for institutions and particularly investment funds looking to buy or sell large positions. By using an automated VWAP strategy, they can track the market without taking sizeable losses.

Execution at or close to VWAP works best for large liquid stocks with tight spreads. Some brokerages offer guaranteed VWAP executions for their clients, but these tend to be only for heavily traded stocks. Refer to Chapter 3 for more information about VWAP.

Participation rate

In a *participation rate* strategy, a trade is entered based on a certain percentage of the average volume. This differs to the VWAP in that the trading program (or the trader manually) chooses a constant participation rate that won't have too much of an impact on the price.

For example, if a trader thinks a 5 per cent participation is appropriate, the program will only enter orders up to 5 per cent of the overall volume.

Dark

Dark algorithms operate solely in dark pools, completely excluding and bypassing the lit markets. These strategies can be any or a variation of VWAP, implementation shortfall or participation rate strategies.

A bank that runs its own dark pool might operate dark algorithms that operate solely on its own dark pool, or a broker dealer may have an algorithm that searches several dark pools for liquidity.

Implementation shortfall

The price of a stock when the decision to invest is made is seldom the same as the price at which the stock can be traded. The difference between the price at the time of the investment decision (*arrival price*) to the execution price (included commissions) is called the *implementation shortfall*. Implementation shortfall strategies attempt to minimise the difference between the two prices by adjusting trade volume (participation rate) based on the price. If the stock trades at below the arrival price, the algorithm gobbles up as much as it can of the volume on offer. If, however, the stock trades above the arrival price then only small trades, or none at all, are done.

Implementation shortfall strategies are used for trades that have high priority and need to be executed quickly. In general the best time to use an implementation shortfall strategy is early in the trading day in the United States and in the afternoons in Europe when there tends to be more liquidity on offer.

The benchmark for implementation shortfall strategies is set when the decision to invest is made. The benchmark price doesn't change; hence limit orders are often necessary and therefore liquidity is important for a successful trade. There is always a risk that the trade won't get filled due to a static benchmark. Implementation shortfall strategies often necessitate the use of dark pools when looking for liquidity.

I can't stress enough the need for speed and low latency. The speed at which information travels from one place to another is of significant importance when it comes to automated trading. Information can't travel faster than the speed of light, which puts a limit between reporting information in one place and the information being received in another.

For instance, New York is home to the New York Stock Exchange (NYSE), NASDAQ and Wall Street. Chicago is home to the American futures and options market. A distance of 730 miles separates the two cities. The speed of light between the two cities is 13.5 milliseconds. Currently, it takes about 15 milliseconds to send information via ultra-low latency channels from one city to the other. Current technology is therefore coming close to the top speed limit of information transfer.

Those with access to that kind of speed of access are obviously at an advantage, but they need more than just speed. Speed is only the time it takes the information to reach one place, but there is still the issue of latency. Remember latency? From a trigger to an action?

The latency loop

The receiving of the information is only the trigger that sets in motion a computer algorithm that has to process several decisions that at best can take as little as a few fractions of a millisecond; even so this still takes time. I will refer to it here as the *latency loop*. Here are the six steps involved in a latency loop:

1. **Analyse the incoming information.**

   The information is analysed based on the criteria you have programmed into your algorithm. The algorithm is designed to follow certain criteria, such as incoming order size, news flow and bid-offer spread.

2. **Take action based on your analysis.**

   The analysis should bring about a decision on the action to take. There are four choices of action open to the algorithm based on the analysis. You can

   - **Buy:** If the decision is one that predicts a rise in the price of the stock then the decision should be to buy.

   - **Sell:** If the decision is one that predicts a decrease in the price of the stock then the decision should be to sell.

   - **Hold:** If the analysed news doesn't have an effect on the stock price, you should hold the existing position and not enter a new position.

   - **Do nothing:** At first this may seem irrelevant, but from a computer programming point of view doing nothing is also an action. It differs from the 'Hold' decision in that if the stock is not in the trader's portfolio, a decision on doing nothing means not entering a trade.

3. **If you buy or sell, determine how much.**

   The amount to buy or sell is dependent on the available volume at that particular time. It's no good coming up with an order to buy 10,000 shares if only 100 are offered at the price your algorithm deems suitable.

4. **Send the order.**

   After the algorithm confirms the analysis, decision and ability to execute the trade, the algorithm has to send the order to the market.

5. **Wait for execution and confirmation.**

   For further trading to continue, your algorithm needs to receive confirmation that a trade is executed so that it's aware of your positions and can continue to operate effectively and continue analysing and sending orders to the market.

This is the last step of the latency loop before beginning again. Information and data is constantly monitored by the algorithm to assess whether there is an event that would trigger a purchase or a sale of stock.

6. **Begin the process again.**

The algorithm is programmed to automatically begin the process again from the first step of analysing incoming data and making a decision as to whether to buy, sell, hold or do nothing.

This process continues, constantly adding more information to the algorithms database as orders are executed and continue to go through this cycle. The latency loop can take several milliseconds, depending on the complexity of the program, the speed of the network and how well the program communicates with the exchange and/or intermediary broker.

Chapter 8

Grasping Standard Order Types

*K*nowing how to place an order and, more importantly, knowing what type of order you should be placing in the market are important pieces of information to have when investing in dark pools. Order types can be categorised in two ways:

✔ Standard order types, also sometimes referred to as traditional order types, which I discuss in this chapter

✔ New special order types, which I cover in Chapter 9

Each type of standard order is treated differently when it enters the market and each order affects the order book in different ways. If you happen to be using the wrong type of order, it can be costly to you in terms of either paying a higher price than you expected to, selling at a lower price than you hoped, missing the trade completely or just getting a partial fill.

There are only a handful of traditional order types and all special order types are derived from the traditional ones. The traditional orders are as follows:

✔ At-market order

✔ Limit order

✔ Stop order

✔ Iceberg order

✔ Fill or kill order (FOK)

✔ Immediate order, also referred to as a cancel order, or immediate or cancel (IOC)

This chapter examines these types in greater detail so you know exactly how your order interacts with the market and what conditions apply to each order. Standard and special order types are right at the heart of dark pools and high frequency trading (HFT). You have to have a handle on the standard order types so that you can also understand how special order types help high frequency traders in their trading.

By knowing how standard order types work and how to use them, you can be best equipped to choose the right type of order for your trade. Standard order types originate from the displayed markets, but because your orders may also be routed through dark pools, these orders are also used in dark pools.

Identifying the Standard Order Types

Standard order types were around long before dark pools and HFT. These sections show you how the different standard order types work and why you need a good grasp of them in order to understand the workings of dark pools and HFT.

Comprehending price time priority

Before delving into the standard order types, you need to have be able to comprehend the concept of price time priority. Price time priority is paramount to understanding how orders are placed in the order book and it's also one of the basic principles under which stock markets work (and so should dark pools). *Price time priority* simply means that any orders coming into a market are prioritised first by price and then by time. The concept has been at the core of exchange markets since inception and it guarantees an orderly and fair market.

This is how price time priority works. For example, you want to place an order to buy 400 shares at a limit of $49.90. Before you place your order this is how the order book looks. Notice the 600 shares already bid at $49.90.

Size	*Bid*	*Offer*	*Size*
300	50.00	50.10	100
100	49.95	50.15	200
600	49.90	50.20	10,000
500	49.85	50.25	500
100	49.80	50.30	100

You then place your order to buy 400 shares at $49.90, which adds on to the 600 shares already at that price in the book. Now the book looks like this:

Size	Bid	Offer	Size
300	50.00	50.10	100
100	49.95	50.15	200
1,000	49.90	50.20	10,000
500	49.85	50.25	500
100	49.80	50.30	100

The 600 shares that were in the book before will be in front of you if and when they get to be best bid. They may be one order of 600 shares or several orders from different traders, adding up to a total of 600 shares, but all those will be executed before your order at the same price because they entered the book prior to you. Remember the order of importance: first price (which in this example is equal) and then time. If someone were to come into the market with another order at the same price, she would then be put in the queue after you.

Later, in the 'Identifying Advanced Standard Order Types' section in this chapter, I discuss how new orders specially set up for high frequency traders have come to test this basic principle and convinced many market participants that the market is unfair.

Gobbling up everything: At-market orders

The most common type of order is the at-market order. This kind is the Pac-Man of markets. Remember that 1980s' computer arcade game? An at-market order gobbles up whatever in front of it. An *at-market order* (sometimes referred to as *hitting the bid* or *hitting the offer*, depending on whether you're buying or selling) means that you're willing to buy or sell at whatever the going rate is; in other words, at the prevailing market price, hence the name *at market*. An at-market order basically clears the order book. This type of order is the best possible one for you if you find yourself in a hurry and need to close the trade quickly.

Using at-market orders does have some associated risks. They can send the message to the market that you're desperate to get a hold of the stock and are willing to buy it at any price. From the preceding example, an at-market order can move the price of a stock significantly. Instead, sometimes being patient and waiting can be more economical. It's possible that some trader will come into the market with a new offer after you've bought your first shares.

For an individual private investor buying a few hundred shares every now and then and paying a few cents above the current market price to get an execution isn't that costly. However, for traders doing large volume trades or institutions buying large blocks of shares a few cents can add up to significant money.

Many traders and investors believe that at-market orders are fodder for high frequency traders. If you have seen the price of the equities slide against you when placing an at-market order, followed by an execution at a different price from where the market was when you placed your order – and a worse price for you – the likelihood is that high frequency traders are trading in that stock. *Slippage* is the difference in the price when you place the order and what price you receive at execution. If you consistently find that your orders are suffering from significant slippage, I advise that you avoid using at-market orders with that stock. To counteract, use a limit order (which I discuss in the next section).

To understand how at-market orders work, consider this simple example that has no hidden orders in the book. (If there are hidden orders then they're called iceberg orders. Refer to the later section 'Hiding behind the full amount: Iceberg orders' for more information about these types of orders.) The following table shows the current market for Acme, Inc. As you can see, it's bid at $50.00 and offered at $50.10. The term *size* refers to the amount of shares that a buyer is willing to buy on the bid side and the amount of shares a seller is willing to sell on the offer side. You want to buy 100 shares, and you want them now. You log in to your trading account and enter the order as *at market* and send it to the market. You would get those 100 shares at $50.10 per share (a total of $5,010 plus commission), provided of course that no other order at a better price gets in front of you before your trade is executed. Your order would be executed against the 100 shares offered at $50.10 in the book, which is the lowest possible offer price that is always first in the order book.

Size	Bid	Offer	Size
300	50.00	50.10	100
100	49.95	50.15	200
600	49.90	50.20	10,000
500	49.85	50.25	500
100	49.80	50.30	100

On your own trading screen you wouldn't even see your order; you would simply see the 100 shares at $50.10 disappear when your order is matched against it, and the order book would change to reflect the trade to look like the following table. As you can see, the $50.10 was taken out by your order and now the best offer is $50.15.

Size	Bid	Offer	Size
300	50.00	50.15	200
100	49.95	50.20	10,000
600	49.90	50.25	500
500	49.85	50.30	100
100	49.80		

I understand that so far these are basic examples, so consider what happens if you want to buy more shares.

Look at the first table and pretend you're extra hungry for Acme, Inc. shares. Instead of wanting 100 shares, you now want to go all in and buy 500 shares and you want them right now. You enter your trade and here is what happens in the order book.

Size	Bid	Offer	Size
300	50.00	50.10	100
100	49.95	50.15	200
600	49.90	50.20	10,000
500	49.85	50.25	500
100	49.80	50.30	100

You first get the 100 shares at $50.10, followed by 200 shares at $50.15 and finally the remaining 200 at $50.20, for a grand total of $25,080 (plus commission), which comes out at an average price per share of $50.16.

After your big purchase, the order book would look like this:

Size	Bid	Offer	Size
300	50.00	50.20	9,800
100	49.95	50.25	500
600	49.90	50.30	100
500	49.85		
100	49.80		

The 100 shares at $50.10 and 200 shares at $50.15 have disappeared, and 200 shares from the offer of 10,000 shares have gone to you and the remaining 9,800 are now the best offer at $50.20.

Setting the price on a matching trade: Limit orders

Limit orders are the second most common order type of orders. As the name suggests, with a *limit order* you place an order where you set the price (limit) at which you'll accept a matching trade. Essentially, you're telling your broker and the market the maximum price that you're willing to buy at or the minimum price that you're willing to sell at. Algorithmic trading programs – and particularly HFT programs – make calculations based on the depth and contents of the order book.

A good way to test to see whether high frequency traders are operating in your stock is to place a limit order a few pegs down the order book and then see whether new orders enter the book immediately after you've entered your order. Then cancel your order and see whether those shares disappear again. Doing so tells you whether an algorithm is trading in the stock.

If the stock is very liquid and volatile, you could have your order executed, so only try this procedure in a stock that you're planning to buy anyway. You can use this test to gauge the level at which you want to place your order.

Consider this example. Look at how such an order looks in the order book. In fact, the order book is made up of limit orders. They give you a picture of the market. This table shows how the market looks now:

Size	Bid	Offer	Size
300	50.00	50.10	100
100	49.95	50.15	200
600	49.90	50.20	10,000
500	49.85	50.25	500
100	49.80	50.30	100

You want to buy 400 shares, but you don't want to pay a cent more than $49.90. That's why when you place your bid order you enter 400 shares and set a limit price of $49.90.

When your order hits the market, the order book looks like this:

Size	Bid	Offer	Size
300	50.00	50.10	100
100	49.95	50.15	200
1,000	49.90	50.20	10,000
500	49.85	50.25	500
100	49.80	50.30	100

As you can see, your 400 shares have been added to the previous 600 shares that were already in the book at $49.90, so now the order book has a 1,000 shares all together bid at $49.90.

If someone were to come into the market and send an at-market order to sell 400 shares (or a limit order to sell 400 shares at a limit of $49.95), the 1,000 shares at $49.90 (including your 400 shares) would then rise to the top and become the best bid, because the 300 shares at $50.00 and the 100 shares at $49.95 would be taken out, as shown:

Size	Bid	Offer	Size
1,000	49.90	50.10	100
500	49.85	50.15	200
100	49.80	50.20	10,000
		50.25	500
		50.30	100

Managing risk: Stop orders

A *stop order* is a specific type of order that you use to manage risk. You place a stop order at a price that is currently worse for you than the prevailing market price, and it doesn't show in the order book.

You may wonder why you or anyone else would want to go the stop order route. You or others use stop orders because they aren't immediately executed because of the following:

- ✔ You can't have a crossed market in which an offer is lower than a bid. This is against the rules on all exchanges.
- ✔ Because the prevailing prices in the book would be better than your order, your trade would be executed at those better prices.

So why would you want to place an order that would be executed at a price that is worse than the current price? Think of it as a form of insurance. The stock can still go up, but you fear an overall market correction and want to protect your investment and set a limit.

Always be careful when placing stop orders because there is no guarantee of execution at the price you want.

For example, say you have bought some Acme, Inc. shares a year ago at $35.00 and now it's trading at around $50.00. You're sitting on a nice profit and would like to protect your profit, but you also think there may be some upside left in the stock and don't want to get out too early. You can then instruct your broker to put your order as a stop order.

You could place your stop at, for example, $45.00, and if there is a drop in the price of the shares, you still have the potential to get out of the trade at a profit.

Potential means that if the price falls to $45.00 and your stop is triggered, provided there is enough buying volume above your purchase price and at or below your stop of $45.00, you'll get out of the trade at a profit. The stop was placed at $45.00, so you may think that you're guaranteed a price of $45.00. However, you aren't, and many investors often overlook this part of a stop order. If the price of the stock hits your stop limit, the order becomes an at-market order. Therefore you aren't guaranteed in any way getting the order filled at the price of the stop.

If the stock significantly drops or the stock or market crashes, it can be particularly disappointing for you and your stop order. When such an event occurs, the liquidity can simply disappear and all or most of the bids can disappear as traders cancel their orders. As a result, after the price crashes through your stop, there may not be anyone at that level, or even several levels below, who is willing to buy your sell order, which is now an at-market order.

As the price proceeds to fall, you'll only be executed when there is a matching buy order for your sell order – either another order to buy at market or to buy at a limit of well below your stop. A crash situation will inevitably have an oversupply of at-market sell orders and a lack of limit orders and at-market orders to buy, resulting in a fast move downward in the stock.

Ask your broker whether she accepts stop orders, because some brokers still don't. Also ask how your broker handles stop orders. Some still handle them manually, in which case you aren't guaranteed that the stop will even be placed. If the broker handling the stock happens to be out for lunch when the stop price is hit then the order won't be placed and you'll get some kind of excuse from your broker. The broker won't make her commission, but you on the other hand will be much worse off without having your stop activated and thus losing out on an execution of your trade. When it comes to stops, a broker who uses an algorithm is your friend. If your broker has a program that places and executes your stop instead of doing it manually, your chance of a quick execution in your stop order is much more likely.

Stop orders aren't only for protecting profits. A professional trader always prefers a small loss to a big loss, so she'll often enter a stop order immediately after entering a position. For example, if a trader buys 100 Acme, Inc. stock at $50.00, she may place a stop order to sell at $49.50 in case the trade turns against her. When a stop order is used in this way, to minimise a loss and not to protect a profit, it is referred to as a *stop-loss* order.

Identifying Advanced Standard Order Types

You need to be aware of a few advanced standard order types. Institutions and professional traders trying to execute larger positions commonly use these types of orders. Many trading algorithms are designed to execute these types of orders, by hiding the total volume and breaking the order up into smaller baby orders. High frequency traders use algorithms to fish out these types of large, hidden orders and trade against them. Finding these hidden orders and then trading against them is how many high frequency traders try to make their money.

If you have an order that is large compared to the average order in that stock, knowing how these orders can be used can help you in your investing. If you're representing an institutional investor and are responsible for executing stock orders, you need to know how these advanced orders can help you in keeping the price steady and not have it move against you while you're trying to complete your order.

Hiding behind the full amount: Iceberg orders

An *iceberg order* is an order that doesn't show the full amount of the order in the order book. They're commonly executed using an algorithm. Because they only show a part of the order and the rest of the order is hidden, they're called iceberg orders: the tip of the iceberg is all you can see.

The risk with an iceberg order is that the price will move against you and your order won't be filled or you'll be left with only a partial fill. High frequency traders often look for iceberg orders because large investors also commonly use them. An iceberg order in the market means there is a large buyer or seller in that stock; it may be that it's trying to fill the order throughout the day at as favourable a price as possible, but that it also has a deadline. For example, an investment fund may have a large withdrawal from a client and therefore need to liquidate some positions to generate cash. In such a case, the fund will eventually have to make the trade regardless of price. Knowing this gives you an opportunity to trade ahead of that order and then profit when the fund eventually has to execute the full order.

Trading via a dark pool is an alternative to trading with an iceberg order, but because high frequency traders have been allowed into some dark pools, they have found ways of sniffing out large dark pool orders as well, and therefore some dark pools have implemented iceberg types of orders.

Derivatives of iceberg orders on offer are based on a benchmark. For example, the Volume Weight Adjusted Price (VWAP) and the price at which your shares will be shown on the market change based on the VWAP. These kinds of orders are executed via algorithms.

Here is an example of an iceberg order. You're the trader for a pension fund and receive orders from the portfolio manager to liquidate 50,000 shares in Acme, Inc. as soon as possible, but without alerting the market. You have a look at the market and it looks like this:

Size	*Bid*	*Offer*	*Size*
300	50.00	50.10	100
100	49.95	50.15	200
600	49.90	50.20	10,000
500	49.85	50.25	500
100	49.80	50.30	100

If you place an at-market order, the price will fall and you have no idea by how much. If you add up all the shares showing in the bid side, you can see for definite (iceberg orders may be hidden there as well) that there are 1,600 shares in total. That level is nowhere near the amount of shares you want to sell.

So what can you do? Your order, if entered into the market in full and without a limit, will send the price down and execute against all the volume showing on the order book at the time and any other orders below that. Because you want as small an effect as possible on the price, the best thing for you to do is to place an iceberg order. Whenever you don't want to move the price, but you know the size of your trade is so big that it would move the price based on what is in the order book, you should use an iceberg order. In the previous example you could go inside the current spread with an iceberg sell order showing only 1,000 shares at a time at a price of $50.05. The order book would then look like this:

Size	*Bid*	*Offer*	*Size*
300	50.00	50.05	1,000
100	49.95	50.10	100
600	49.90	50.15	200
500	49.85	50.20	10,000
100	49.80	50.25	500

Here the order book, on the offer side, shows 1,000 of your shares for sale at $50.05, so now your best offer, the remaining 49,000 shares you want to sell, is in fact hidden from the order book. If anyone comes in with an at-market order or limit order to buy at $50.05, you sell 1,000 shares and would now have 49,000 left to sell. Immediately after the sale of your 1,000 shares, a new order of 1,000 shows up on the offer at the price of $50.05. This continues until all your 50,000 shares are sold. Because you instructed to show 1,000 shares at a time, each time 1,000 are sold a new lot of 1,000 pops up in the trading book.

Wanting it now: Fill or kill orders

A *fill or kill order* (FOK) is used when you absolutely have to get the full quantity of an order filled at a specific price. Some HFT orders are derivatives of fill or kill orders. Some traders will use FOK orders to find hidden orders in the market. Also, some traders use them when there is a specific amount of shares and a price they're looking for when trading.

Using a FOK order does have its risks. You may be left without any shares at all, but for most active traders this risk isn't an issue because they tend to have an exact entry point and an exact exit point planned before placing any order. If they miss a trade, there will always be another one along soon. Notice that the risk with a FOK order is minimal when entering a position; the worst thing that will happen is that you miss a trade, but you won't lose any money. There is a risk, however, if you have an open position and are trying to get out of it; with a FOK order you might not get your trade executed and you'll still be left with an open position with perhaps a market moving against you with the losses adding up. That's why FOK orders are better used as entry orders.

To see how a FOK order works, say that you're an active day trader and are looking to make a quick in/out profit on Acme, Inc. You want to buy 2,000 shares at $50.05, but when you look at the order book there are only 1,000 showing at your price. Of course, there may be an iceberg order in the market, as mentioned in the earlier section, 'Hiding behind the full amount: Iceberg orders'. Now you can fish out that order and see whether there is in fact hidden volume behind the 1,000 shares shown at $50.05 by placing a FOK order. Refer to this table:

Size	Bid	Offer	Size
300	50.00	50.05	1,000
100	49.95	50.10	100
600	49.90	50.15	200
500	49.85	50.20	10,000
100	49.80	50.25	500

When you place the order, you get the whole order filled, the 2,000 shares, because an iceberg order is in the market. If on the other hand, there really were only 1,000 shares on offer and no hidden iceberg order, you would get zero shares. The whole point of a FOK order is to get each and every share you want.

Executing only a portion: Immediate or cancel orders

The immediate or cancel order (IOC) is very similar to an FOK order. Under normal conditions, when you place an order in the market, it's in for the duration of the trading day. An IOC order differs from an FOK order in that if only a portion of the volume can be executed, it will be. With a FOK order both the price and all the volume have to be matched for the order to be completed. An IOC order will enter the market and try to fill all the order; if there isn't enough volume at that limit to complete the order then it will execute all the volume it can and cancel the remaining order. IOC orders are sent out one time and get either fully or partially filled, but they're always immediately cancelled after they hit the market.

High frequency traders use IOC orders to sniff out larger orders; by sending out IOC orders an algorithm can gain information about hidden volume in the market.

Say, for example, the order book looks like the one shown in the following table. You place an order to buy 1,500 shares in Acme, Inc. at $50.05 (assuming there is no hidden volume) and you make it an IOC order. You get only 1,000 shares, and instead of your remaining 500 shares now becoming the best bid at $50.05 they're cancelled. You have to enter a new order if you want to buy more.

Size	Bid	Offer	Size
300	50.00	50.05	1,000
100	49.95	50.10	100
600	49.90	50.15	200
500	49.85	50.20	10,000
100	49.80	50.25	500

Chapter 9

Identifying the Special Order Types

*T*his chapter focuses on the most contentious thing in algorithmic and high frequency trading (HFT) – the special order types. Nothing brings about a more heated discussion about HFT than special order types. Some market participants are convinced that these types are unfair and a conspiracy against the investor. Others who support HFT argue that these types are just another form of market evolution that take into account the use of algorithmic trading, improve on market structure and are the best friend of the investor in the form of tighter spreads.

All special order types are derived from the traditional order types. If you aren't aware of the standard order types, such as at market, limit and iceberg, I suggest that you check out Chapter 8.

Getting a Hold of the Basics of Special Order Types

Special order types have been shrouded in mystery because they tend to be orders that can only be executed via computer trading models. If you log in to your own trading account and choose the order type, it's highly unlikely that any of the special order types will be made available to you.

That doesn't mean you can't and don't have a right to use them. Relevant financial authorities, such as the Securities and Exchanges Commission (SEC) in the United States, must approve order types, so in theory special order types are open to all investors trading on the exchange in question.

The problem is that they can be confusing and not publicly promoted by the exchange. These sections explain some common traits of special orders and the difference between routable and non-routable orders.

Eyeing their characteristics

Special order types are constantly being added to and changed. Anything written on a particular special order type runs the risk of being out of date as new special order types are brought in. Not to worry, though, because a couple of aspects of special order types remain constant, regardless of the order type. They all tend to be a combination of two things:

- **Hidden volume:** Although the order is active on the market, some or all of the volume isn't visible on the order book.

- **The way they interact within the bid-offer spread:** The order's position in the order book queue and when it becomes active or visible is dependent on the bid-offer spread.

Exchanges keep coming up with the most imaginative ways of combining these two aspects to offer sophisticated traders ways to place orders in the market. The good news is that you don't need to remember each and every special order by heart, but having a simple understanding of how special order types work and are set up can help you decide whether these types of orders are right for you and how they affect your own orders.

An individual special order type tends to be one or a combination of these three characteristics:

- **Pegged:** The order is based on a benchmark bid-offer and moves when the bid-offer changes.

- **Hidden:** Some or all of the volume in the order isn't shown on the order book.

- **Post only:** An order designed to gain rebates and add liquidity. If there is a matching order in the market, a post-only order would slide a price point away so that it wouldn't execute.

All special order types include one or all three of these characteristics. Each exchange or dark pool has its own specific special orders with their own names. It can get a little confusing because special order types are complex with many different attributes. If you keep in mind that at their root they tend to be a combination of pegged, hidden and post-only orders then you'll be able to work them out.

The order types and how they interact with the market for a single exchange would be enough to fill a book of its own, so the rest of this chapter concentrates on the common terms and features across all market venues so you can understand how they work.

The US markets, with their multitude of different venues, both lit and dark, and with their Regulation New Market System (Reg NMS) and their ban on locked markets, are the most complex. After you have an understanding of how they work, figuring out how to understand other markets (such as the European market) will be simple. So with that in mind, the majority of this chapter (unless otherwise stated) refers to special order types used in the United States.

Differentiating between routable and non-routable orders

A single company's stock can trade on several displayed stock exchanges (and numerous dark pools), which means that the best possible price might be on a different exchange or dark pool to the exchange you or your broker sends the order to. That's why orders are *routed* to the venue with the best available price so that you can get the best possible price. You would think this would be the best possible outcome in all situations, but that's not so. In some situations having an order that isn't routed to another exchange is preferable when you're in search of a better price. That situation is particularly relevant when there are rebates involved. The ability to route or not to route an order is the reason that so many special orders types have been created.

In a nutshell, the two terms mean the following:

- **Routable:** If you place an order with your broker who then places the order at the venue of his choice and there's a better price available in a dark pool or competing exchange, your broker can move the money to another exchange or dark pool and execute it there. The good news is that the default for a standard order is that it is routable. It'll go through and find the best available price at the time and execute against that price.

- **Non-routable:** This method comes down to money and rebates. Some market makers and HFT specialist firms receive a rebate for providing liquidity, which means placing limit bids and offers on the book of the exchange. If a matching order comes into the market then the broker gets a small rebate from the exchange. This practice of paying rebates to liquidity providers is often referred to as a *maker fee.*

What may appear confusing is that some exchanges have *taker* rebates, which are rebates for those who take liquidity. An at-market order is a liquidity-taking order, and so is any limit order entering the market that takes out the current best bid or offer.

A firm that has a maker fee agreement with one exchange and a taker fee with another can, in theory, after pocketing a maker fee turn around (in milliseconds) and liquidate that position at the exact same price in a market that pays it a taker fee. This way the firm can pocket two rebates in a round trip on one single stock. Good business if you can get it. The subject of maker/taker fees is one of controversy; some investors and market commentators feel that maker/taker fees are unfair and even unethical.

Knowing whether an order is routed or not is relevant. It has to do with the rule on locked markets. If a non-routable order can be matched in another market (an *away market*) when posted on the book, it would lock the market. This is a no-no and isn't allowed because of the rule on locked markets. An equal price bid on one market and offer on another market is banned because it's against the principle of an orderly market. In an orderly market, these two should be matched.

Providing Firms with Rebates: Post-Only Orders

HFT firms specifically created the post-only order types, which are unique to algorithmic trading. These orders can supply the firms with rebates. Exchanges and dark pools like to pay rebates to those traders who can bring liquidity to their markets, with the idea that the more liquidity there is, the more trades get matched, and every matched trade results in a fee for the exchange. Liquidity is provided by limit orders. The more limit orders (particularly visible ones) there are, the more liquidity is believed to be in the market.

When a *post-only order* enters the market, even if there's a matching order that would execute against it, it isn't matched. It's simply posted on the book. You may wonder why someone would post an order if it weren't executed when there is a matching order. When a rebate is added to the mix, it suddenly starts to make sense.

When you send a limit order into the market, you're said to be providing liquidity. You're showing your hand, saying, 'I will buy (or sell) at this price. Here is my order; come and take it.' You're sitting there on the book for all to see, showing how much you'll do of what and at what price. You're therefore giving or providing liquidity.

When an order comes into the market that matches the price of your limit order, your order and the matching order obviously disappear, because they'll be executed against each other and the deal will have been done. The incoming order matched against yours and it just took away the liquidity you gave to the market. This is referred to as *taking liquidity*.

Some exchanges pay rebates to those traders who provide liquidity (many high frequency traders' business models are based on catching rebates). If a trader is providing liquidity and she knows that she is going to get a rebate, it would come as an unpleasant shock if when she posted a limit order she discovered that there was some hidden volume that immediately matched against her order. The trader thought she was providing liquidity; instead she had been taking it. Now the trader has two problems:

- ✔ She's entered a trade that she didn't want to get into in the first place.
- ✔ She hasn't even received a rebate. Because she took the liquidity, she's actually paying the fee.

A post-only order is never routed, and it has a special provision to never be executed if on entering the market there is already an existing matching order on the opposite side. It's purely there to catch the rebate.

Unless you're an institutional trader, it's highly unlikely that your broker/ exchange will ever suggest that you use a post-only order.

Moving to the Next Level: Hide and Not Slide Orders

The *hide and not slide order*, one of the more common special order types, is one for the US markets. To understand how it works, remember the regulatory ban on locked markets: if a trader sends an order into the market at a limit price and it's a non-routable order (only to be executed in the exchange the order is entered into) and an existing matching order already exists in another market (an *away market*) then it would lock the market, which isn't allowed.

In such a case, the order would *slide*, meaning that it would move to the next price level to wait for the matching order in the other market to be taken out, in which case the order would slide back to its original price. However, there's a sneaky little trick used by high frequency traders called the *hide not slide order* in which they can actually jump in front of your order.

Here's an example of the hide not slide order in action. The current best bid and offer in the markets look like this:

Size	Bid	Offer	Size
300	50.09	50.10	100

You send a non-routable order to buy 100 shares of Acme, Inc. at $50.10. Because an offer at that price already exists in another market, posting your order causes a locked market. Your order can't be shown, so it slides to $50.09. That's right, it slides. No one asks your permission because locked markets are banned, and as a result your bid price is now lower.

Now immediately after you another trader posts a hide not slide order to buy 200 shares at $50.10. This order is not displayed because, as the first part of the order indicates, it hides. The ban on locked markets only affects posted orders, so this hidden order doesn't lock the market. As the second part of the order indicates, it doesn't slide. So there it sits, hidden from view. You won't see it and other market participants won't see it, but there it is.

You may wonder what the point of this order is. When the offer side of 100 shares at $50.10 gets taken out, the market is no longer locked and the hide not slide order pops up like a cork out of water on the bid side at $50.10. The top of the book will now look like this:

Size	Bid	Offer	Size
300	50.10	50.11	200

You may wonder what happened to your order. Your order of 100 shares slides back to its original $50.10, and it goes in the queue behind the hide not slide order of 200 shares. So although the order is placed after yours, the hide not slide order gets a place in front of you. (The order doesn't follow *price/time priority*, which means that the first order to come into the market at a particular price is the first in the queue. Refer to Chapter 8 for more information on price/time priority.)

If you're considering using hide not slide orders, you need to be aware that most equities move at a pace so quick that your eyes won't be able to follow them in order to take advantage of these discrepancies. Using these types of orders in very slow moving stocks is possible, but the benefit with these kinds of stocks is probably only a few pennies in price, so your overall price won't really be affected unless your turnover of trades is huge.

Hide not slide orders are controversial. Those who oppose them argue that they violate the principle of price/time priority by allowing certain market participants to queue-jump. Regulators are having an ongoing debate as to whether hide not slide orders should be banned.

Getting the Best Possible Price: Peg Orders

Peg orders are used in fast-moving and volatile markets and give the trader the possibility of getting the best possible price. The price in a peg order moves within certain boundaries. When entering a peg order, depending on the type of peg order, the price is based on the National Best Bid Offer (NBBO).

The National Best Bid (NBB) is a consolidated price from all the national stock exchanges with the highest price someone is willing to buy the stock. The National Best Offer (NBO) is the lowest price someone is willing to sell the stock for. Often you will see the National Best Bid Offer (NBBO) mentioned, and this refers to the spread, the price difference between the NBB and the NBO.

Peg orders are divided into three common types:

- ✔ Primary peg orders
- ✔ Market peg orders
- ✔ Midpoint peg orders

The following sections take a closer look at these three types of peg orders.

Lining up first: Primary peg orders

Primary peg orders, also referred to as *regular peg orders*, are always pegged to the same side of the order book (the bid or the offer), so if you want to buy a stock, it's pegged to the bid side, and if you want to sell a stock, it's pegged to the offer side. These orders follow the best bid when you're buying and the best offer when you're selling. The good thing about a primary peg order is that it allows you to look for the best possible price. You place a limit on your peg, which is the highest price that you're willing to buy at (lowest to sell), but instead of showing the highest price that you're willing to buy at, the primary peg order only displays with the best bid. Therefore, if someone comes into the market with an at-market order to sell, for example, you get a better price than your highest limit, provided of course that the best bid at the time is below your maximum limit.

To really understand how primary peg orders work, check out this example. You want to buy 200 shares of Acme, Inc., and the highest you're willing to pay is $50.40, but currently the market looks like this:

NBB	*NBO*
50.00	50.50

You place a primary peg order to buy the 200 shares at a limit of $50.40. Instead of your order moving the NBB to $50.40, your order actually joins the current NBB of $50.00. If another limit order enters the market at $50.10 and becomes the NBB, your order simply slides up to $50.10.

	NBB	*NBO*
50.00	50.10	50.50

These price changes continue to happen all the way up to your limit of $50.40. The primary peg order gives you the possibility to try to get an even better price without having to adjust your limit all the time.

If sitting at the NBB isn't good enough for you and you're feeling a little greedy then you can add an offset to your limit order. This means that when the bid or offer changes (depending on which side your order is pegged to), your price will also change, but it will be at a slight different price (offset) from the bid or offer. This little trick allows you to be first in line all the time. Sticking to the same example, in addition to making the primary peg order you add an offset of one cent, $0.01. Provided that your limit isn't reached, your order will be $0.01 ahead of any bid that comes in. Basically, this type of order allows you to be on the NBB, first in line, all the time. With your order of $50.01, it looks like this:

NBB	*NBO*
50.00	50.50

If the NBB is $50.00 and you place a primary peg order with a limit of $50.40 and an offset of $0.01 then your order becomes the NBBO like this:

	NBB	*NBO*
50.00	50.01	50.50

If someone now came in with a new bid of $50.05, your order would change to $50.06, keeping you nicely in front of the queue waiting for that matching limit or at-market order, such as this:

	NBB	*NBO*
50.05	50.06	50.50

Buying based on offer price and selling based on bid price: Market peg orders

Market peg orders, also known as *reverse peg orders*, work the same as a primary peg orders, except that they follow the opposite side of the spread to the primary peg order. A market peg order buys based on the offer price and sells based on the bid price. When you place a market peg buy order, your price will be pegged to the offer. On the other side, if you place a sell order, your price will be pegged to the bid.

Because the peg follows the opposite (also known as the *contra*) side of the market, a market peg order is more aggressive than the primary peg order.

Matching in the middle: Midpoint peg orders

Midpoint peg orders are floating orders that are matched at the midpoint of the NBBO. The midpoint of the NBBO is the average of the NBB and NBO. Most dark pool orders are based on the midpoint of the NBBO, so these orders are great for fishing out hidden orders and orders in dark pools.

To get the average price between the NBB and NBBO, just use this simple division problem:

$$\frac{NBB + NBO}{2}$$

Midpoint peg orders (sometimes referred to as *pegged to midpoint orders*) are similar to the most common type of dark pool order, which is matched at the average of the best bid and best offer. A midpoint peg order is a non-displayed order that calculates the average price between the best bid and best offer and executes at that price.

A midpoint peg order is used for staying in front of the queue. For example, you want to buy 200 shares of Acme, Inc. and the price bid is $50 and the offer $50.10. You decide to go for a midpoint execution, which would give a price of $50.05. Your order won't be displayed, but it will be executed at the mid-price if there is an at-market sell order, a limit sell order or a limit mid peg sell order. In this example you can see the displayed prices but not the midpoint order, but you can calculate the midpoint price by taking the average of the best bid and the best offer.

Size	Bid	Offer	Size
200	50.00	50.10	1,000
1,000	49.90	50.15	200

If the bid or the offer changes then your order price will also change. Imagine that the best bid of $50.00 is cancelled and the best bid changes to $49.90. Now your midpoint peg order would be priced at the average of $49.90 and 50.10, which is $50.00.

Executing Quickly: Intermarket Sweep Orders (ISOs)

Intermarket sweep orders (ISOs) are unique to the United States and are one of the most difficult types of order to understand. However, they're at the very heart of special order types. ISOs are designed for large institutions posting big orders to execute them as swiftly as possible by allowing them to *sweep* through multiple layers in the order book without having to re-enter new orders.

The ISO order is an exemption that allows an order to avoid the order protection rule, also referred to as the *trade-through rule*. The *order protection rule* states that an order must check all other venues for the best price, but it can be a slow process and sometimes orders change so quickly in different market venues that an execution is difficult to get. That is why Regulation New Market System (Reg NMS) allows for an exemption, which is to trade the order book of just one market without checking the others.

This is how it works. In effect what happens with an ISO is that it first has to match an order against the NBBO. (Remember, the NBBO is always protected.) After it matches an order against the NBBO, it can then sweep through the market it wants without checking other market venues, taking out other levels that aren't protected. The result is often quick execution but not necessarily the best possible price at the time due to the fragmentation of the markets with multiple venues.

Unlike many other order types, the ISO is specifically mentioned and defined in Reg NMS and is based on the order protection rule, which you can read about in Chapter 6. Always remember that the ISO is a special exemption to the order protection rule. Each and every ISO has to be marked and reported to the authorities.

The following example shows how a basic ISO works. I then examine how it works with several market venues.

Say that you want to place a large sell order for Acme, Inc. for 10,000 shares with a limit of $49.85. At that stage the market looks like this:

Size	Bid	Offer	Size
200	50.09	50.10	1,000
1,000	49.95	50.15	200
7,000	49.90	50.20	8,000
3,000	49.85	50.25	500
500	49.80	50.30	1,000

You enter your order, and it goes through the market, taking out the 200 shares at $50.09 followed by the 1,000 shares at $49.95, 7,000 shares at $49.90 and the remaining 1,800 shares at $49.85. Your average sell price is $49.90, which is a little bit above your limit. You're pleased because it seems like a basic limit order and that's because of Reg NMS and the order protection rule.

Adding another market venue shows how an ISO avoids the order protection rule by trading through the book. Figure 9-1 shows the comparison between the two books:

Figure 9-1: Two different market venue order books trading in the same stock.

A

Size	Bid	Offer	Size
200	50.09	50.10	1,000
1,000	49.95	50.15	200
7,000	49.90	50.20	8,000
3,000	49.85	50.25	500
500	49.80	50.30	1,000

B

Size	Bid	Offer	Size
100	50.10	50.11	1,000
2,000	50.08	50.15	200
3,000	50.03	50.20	8,000
6,000	50.00	50.25	500
500	49.99	50.30	1,000

You have the same order to sell 10,000 shares of Acme, Inc. at a limit of $49.85, and your broker places it for you as an ISO into Market A. The NBB, however, can be found in Market B with 100 shares bid at $50.10, and the NBB and the NBO are always protected. Your order is therefore routed to Market B, where it sells 100 shares and takes out the NBB. Because it's an ISO, it can now sweep Market A without having to look for better prices elsewhere.

Look at the previous example with the order in which you're selling 10,000 Acme, Inc. shares at a limit of $49.85. You'll notice that a better average price would have been obtained by continuing the sales in Market B. Selling 10,000 shares there would have achieved an average price of $50.03 as opposed to $49.90 per share in Market A. The total difference in a trade of that size would have been $1,237.00, which is real money. Figure 9-2 shows the trading books of the two different market venues, where you can see that trading in Market B would've given a better overall price for the trade.

Market A

	Shares	Price	Amount
	200	50.09	10,018
	1,000	49.95	49,950
	7,000	49.90	349,300
	1,800	49.85	89,730
Total	10,000		
Average Price	**49.90**		

Market B

	Shares	Price	Amount
	100	50.10	5010
	2,000	50.08	100,160
	3,000	50.03	150,090
	4,900	50.00	245,000
Total	10,000		
Average Price	**50.03**		

Figure 9-2: Average price difference for the sale of 10,000 shares between Market A and Market B.

As long as the trader makes a best effort to take out the existing NBB or NBO, the order can then sweep the market venue at a less favourable price.

After seeing how an ISO works, you may wonder why anyone should ever send out an order that may result in an unfavourable price. A trader surely would avoid this type of order, right?

You may be surprised to discover that a significant amount of the orders entered into the market today are in fact ISOs. On the NASDAQ, about 50 per cent of all orders are ISOs.

Institutional investors and market makers are the sole users of ISOs; retail investors never get a chance to use them. The use of ISOs comes down to speed because of the high speed of information and the fragmentation of markets (several market venues). The NBBO is sometimes referred to as *stale,* meaning that a protected NBB or NBO is in fact old. So when it's hit, there's nothing there. Fulfilling the trade-through rule and constantly chasing the NBBO via many different markets may mean that an order won't be executed. Hence the ISO is perfect for these kinds of situations.

The NBBO tends to slow down in fast moving markets, due to traffic overload, so with an ISO order you have the chance of getting ahead of the market by sweeping your home venue's book. Great stuff for market makers and traders because they can immediately turn this around and trade it to those coming up behind.

Remember that this all happens in milliseconds. When the NBBO is stale, it's not a question of minutes or seconds; it's a question of milliseconds. These orders that are moving through the markets are going at a pace that no human trader could possibly see, let alone react to.

For rather obvious reasons ISO orders are controversial. Some market participants argue that they're a way to get in front of the queue and others argue that they're a necessity to allow institutional traders to fulfil their orders.

Chapter 10

Delving into High Frequency Trading

In This Chapter

▶ Getting a firm hold of what high frequency trading is

▶ Recognising what high frequency traders do

▶ Looking at the future

*H*igh frequency trading (HFT) is a specific subset of algorithmic trading. Whereas large institutions use algorithmic trading to place their orders in the market as a form of order handling and management, high frequency traders use superfast proprietary trading programs to trade in and out of positions, trying to make small profits out of each trade.

Although HFT may appear to be a recent phenomenon based on the growing publicity that it's receiving, in fact it's a natural progression of the markets. Traders and investors have always searched for technological advantages that can be used for profitable investing. Trading has always been at the forefront of technological change, and HFT is a result of the combination of traders looking to make a profit and technology helping them on their way. First came the computers and then the trading algorithms, followed by HFT.

This chapter explains in great detail what HFT is. No other form of trading has caused as much controversy as HFT, and in this chapter you can find out all about what HFT really is – from a proper definition, which is still missing by many who talk about HFT, to what it is that HFT traders do and how they go about their business. HFT came about because of advances in technology, and as a business it's very much dependent on technological advances. Because of HFT's hi-tech nature, this chapter also speculates on what the future may hold for HFT as technology and regulations covering it change.

Tackling the Definition of High Frequency Trading

In many cases, *high frequency trading (HFT)* is simply the use of modern technology to run age-old trading. Technology has improved the speed of trading, and now the computers do the order inputting and the analysis. But behind it all, the same trading strategies apply.

To help you get a firmer understanding of HFT, the following sections examine what HFT is and what high frequency traders do on a day-to-day basis.

Eyeing HFT: What it's all about?

Many people are confused about HFT. Even the definition of HFT is often unclear. This section helps to clarify some of that confusion. Here I define what HFT is at its core. When you have a clear definition of what HFT is, you'll be better equipped to get to grips with how it works and how it interacts in the market.

Estimates of HFT's share of overall trading volume in the markets vary; some say it's as much as 70 per cent. Regardless of what the exact number is, the share is obviously significant. HFT is a big part of today's market, which is why you should have an understanding of what it takes to operate a HFT operation and what those operations do to make their money, because often they make their money from investors such as yourself.

The following section explains the different aspects that are needed to run an effective HFT operation.

Speed: Ramping up the game

The HFT world has often been referred to as an *arm's race*; it's an apt comparison because that's exactly what it is – a race to outspend the competition to get access to the best and most advanced technology.

HFT uses fast data connections to make rapid trades, often exiting a trade within a few seconds or even milliseconds. High frequency traders don't *carry positions overnight*, meaning that they aren't holding any shares at the end of the trading day. High frequency traders are one reason that you see such heavy trading at the end of a trading day when traders close out their positions before the closing bell.

HFT is faster than any human can react. The programs are able to make a trading decision and enter that position within milliseconds and even faster. As HFT has become more popular after the turn of the millennium, it has all but killed off the day trader. A human can't compete with a fast algorithm when it comes time to trade. So don't even try it!

The following aspects can have an impact on speed in HFT:

- ✔ **Newest technology and programs:** High frequency traders and the firms that provide them with the technological tools they need to operate their trading programs constantly have to invest in better and faster systems to have an edge on the competition. The relentless advances in technology mean that new systems are being introduced to the market regularly, and these systems require new investment from HFT operators. The costs add up and they add up quickly.

- ✔ **Vast investments:** Big money is involved in HFT, which means that the technology involved is state of the art. This technology more often than not is extremely expensive, which is why operating a successful HFT business demands large investments.

- ✔ **Co-location space in the data centre:** *Co-location* means having the HFT firms' servers as close as possible to the trade matching engine of a stock exchange so that trade data has as short as possible a time to travel. (Refer to the next section for more information.)

- ✔ **Best programmers:** These people have the expertise to build algorithms that are fast and accurate. The programmers are the ones who make the trading strategies work in an automated way.

- ✔ **Profitable and reliable trading strategies:** Having the fastest computers and the best programmers is no good if you don't have a trading strategy that is profitable. Refer to Chapter 11 for some specific strategies for HFT.

So if you don't have the financial muscle to wrestle with the big boys then you had better think twice before getting involved. If you can't afford to be a high frequency trader yourself, that doesn't mean you shouldn't know the ins and outs of how it works.

Co-location: Being close to the action

The primary way for HFT firms to get an edge on other investors is co-location. By placing their computers in data centres provided for by exchanges, high frequency traders can act faster than other investors in executing their trades.

'Location, location, location' is a property business saying, but it works for finance as well. The closer you are to the source of the information, the faster the information travels. In fact, co-location is a business that was born from the demands of high frequency traders. It isn't a cheap game, though. The expense of co-location is high and is one of the contributing factors to the decrease in profitability of HFT in recent years.

With ever more competition and the big players all having the same speed, high frequency traders are having more of a difficult time in making a profit, which doesn't mean that co-location ceases to be an important part of HFT. If a high frequency trader can't be faster than the competition, the high frequency trader has to be at least as fast. In the world of HFT, participants can't afford not to keep up.

The magic of the black box

In HFT, the *black box* is a synonym for automated trading or algorithmic trading. In other words, the computer runs the trading program. In its most simple form, the black box is the program into which data is first entered, after which the program gives an instruction to buy, sell, hold or not to enter an order. When it instructs to buy or sell, it also instructs at what price and also what type of order type it gives to the market. The black boxes of trading firms are closely guarded secrets – they're what HFT firms make their money with.

Technology is making it easier for investors to gain access to black boxes, which in essence means building your own working trading models. To get started, what you need is a trading idea or system. You should have back-tested your trading idea against previous market movements to see whether your trading strategy has the possibility of making a profit in a real trading environment. The trading idea needs to be turned into computer code that takes in data, analyses it and then gives an order. If you're not capable of coding, find someone who can to put your trading system into a working black box form.

Several languages are used for algorithmic programming, and one black box may use different languages for different parts of the strategy. One language can be used to analyse the data and to come up with the output needed. In the case of trading, this *output* would be the order that is sent to the market. Then a different language is needed to actually send the order to the market based on what language the trading venue in question uses.

The most common languages for the black box are C#, C++ and Java, although plenty of other languages are also used. (If you want to get to grips with any of these languages, check out the corresponding books in the *For Dummies* series by visiting www.dummies.com.) The black box is of little use to you if it's not fast. In today's markets, opportunities may well be gone if the action from trading opportunity to execution is too slow.

Different languages are used in sending an order to the market. Increasingly, one language has become the most common for communication between different market participants including the exchanges, the buy-side and the sell-side. This language is the FIX algorithmic trading definition language known as FIXatdl. It relies on the FIX protocol, which is a system that allows financial firms and exchanges to communicate with each other in real time. The FIXatdl gives all the necessary output from the black box to the trading venue to place an order in the markets.

Co-location is needed to see, as fast as possible, the orders coming into the market. This information is then fed into the black boxes of high frequency traders that then make the trades (refer to the nearby sidebar about black boxes).

Latency: Reducing time to the minimum

When discussing HFT, latency is an important concept to understand. *Latency* is the whole process from finding out about an event, to analysing the event, to making a decision as to what to do about the event and then to executing that decision. In the case of HFT, the execution of the decision means a completed trade. HFT strives for latency to be as low as possible.

Low latency requires several aspects. Here are three of the most important factors in achieving low latency:

- **Co-location:** Minimises the time it takes for trade data from the stock exchanges servers to get to the computers of the high frequency trader.

- **Direct market access:** Gives a direct line without intermediaries to stock market data.

- **Fast algorithmic programs:** The quicker the program, the quicker an order can be sent out to the market and executed.

Co-location and direct market feeds allow high frequency traders to see what is happening in the market at (near) real time. It also gives them the data that feeds their trading machines, which are the black boxes that house their trading programs. The faster the black box can take in the data, analyse it, come up with an output (a trading instruction) and send it to the market, the better. Good hardware and infrastructure must back up all the data, so when market days get hectic, as they invariably do, the traders are still able to keep going.

Liquidity: Taking or providing it

In many ways the high frequency trader has overtaken the traditional market maker. Due to their constant posting of bids and offers, high frequency traders are often referred to as *liquidity providers. Liquidity provision* is the posting of a bid or an offer with a limit price onto the book of an exchange. Taking liquidity is when an order comes into the market, either as an at-market order or a limit order, and takes out an existing order on the book. Taking liquidity removes an existing order or orders in the trade book. An order will either *take liquidity* or *provide liquidity*. It's not entirely correct to call high frequency traders liquidity providers because they can also be liquidity takers when their trading strategy demands it.

Supporters of HFT claim that it has brought down costs for the investor and reduced spreads. That is certainly true when you take a quick look at any particular stock's order book, but things aren't always as they appear. Although the benevolent appearance of high frequency traders is that they provide all-important liquidity and act as market makers, it's important to remember that they seldom are market makers in the traditional sense (although some are registered as designated market makers).

For example, consider these orders:

Size	*Bid*	*Offer*	*Size*
200	50.09	50.10	1,000

Both orders *provide* liquidity. They are orders on the exchange and can be executed immediately. If an at-market order to buy 1,000 shares comes in then that order will be executed against the offer at $50.10, thus taking the offer out. Hence this at-market order *takes* liquidity. The same would happen if a limit order to sell 200 shares at $50.09 comes into the market. Although it's a limit order, it crosses the spread by taking out the 200 shares at $50.09, thus the limit order is also a liquidity-taking order.

Any limit order on the book that doesn't cross the spread is a liquidity-providing order, and any order that crosses the spread is a liquidity-taking order.

High frequency traders aren't liquidity providers – sometimes they provide liquidity and sometimes they take liquidity, depending on their own trading strategies. They don't have the same responsibilities as designated market makers to act as the buyer of last resort. They can pull out of the market at any time, and they often do.

When a high frequency trader decides to pull her orders in a matter of milliseconds, this can cause problems in the market, particularly in times of strong volatility. Some pundits have blamed the flash crash of 2010 on high frequency traders. At the very least their pulling out of the market contributed to the crash.

Recognising characteristics of high frequency traders

HFT has many different types of strategies and ways of trading. It's not just one thing, but certain characteristics are common to all HFT strategies, and this section explains those characteristics. High frequency traders use a myriad of strategies to do their jobs, which Chapter 11 discusses in greater depth.

High frequency traders are highly sought-after clients for stock exchanges, even for dark pools. Although originally dark pools were meant as a venue for large institutions to escape predatory high frequency traders, the volume of trades they send are exactly what exchanges and dark pools need. They are in fact so sought after that market venues often pay them rebates just so that they trade at their venue.

Here are the main characteristics of high frequency traders:

- ✔ **After they enter a position, they want out as quickly as possible to close it.** High frequency traders make their money on tiny price increments. A tiny price increment means pennies, or even fractions of pennies. Some investors often view high frequency traders as market markers because they try to make the spread by being the first in line at the bid or the offer. To do this requires quick computing power and co-location. Refer to 'Co-location: Being close to the action', earlier in this chapter, for more information.

- ✔ **When buying and selling stocks in large listed firms, they often provide liquidity and tighter spreads.** Doing so benefits the investor, but it's only applicable in normal market conditions. When there is an unusual market event, particularly a crisis, they tend to disappear. For the retail investor, high frequency traders are fickle.

- ✔ **They send out and cancel a large amount of orders.** They do so for several reasons:

  - • Their trading strategies are constantly adjusting to market events as they try to get in and out of a trade. This strategy results in cancellations and inputs of new orders at slightly different prices and/ or volumes.

  - • Sending small orders is a way to try to find information from the market, particularly in trying to find giant orders of hidden volume by sending out small baby orders to test whether they get filled.

  - • Some estimate that over 90 per cent of all orders sent into the market are cancelled. These are high frequency traders in action. So when you see orders in the book and then try to execute a trade at that price, it may not actually happen. Remember that your eyes are way too slow to keep up with the algorithms of high frequency traders.

- ✔ **They display predatory behavior.** With some high frequency traders there might also be some nefarious things going on, such as quote stuffing. (*Quote stuffing* includes both slowing down the exchange and manipulating the price.) For example, by sending out a massive amount of orders, traders can possibly influence price movements in a stock, which gives traders a chance to make profitable trades. Say a high frequency trader wants to sell some shares. She can send out many different buy orders, thus trying to fool other traders into making the assumption that demand for a stock is rising. The fooled traders then start buying the stock, causing an upward price movement. The trader who sent the buy orders then cancels the buy orders and sells the shares she wanted to sell at a higher price.

✔ **They do not hold positions overnight.** High frequency traders tend to go home at night with all their positions closed. They do not hold risk overnight. Their goal is to have as short a holding period for their trades as possible, hopefully getting out of the position immediately after entering it. So after a day of trading against you and taking a bunch of your pennies, the high frequency traders go home and sleep well without fear of having their positions explode on them.

These responsibilities aren't of any use without the appropriate amount of speed. Everything has to be executed in milliseconds and even less. The closer the turnaround is to the speed of light, the happier the high frequency trader is.

Examining what high frequency traders do

To run a HFT operation, certain things need to be present. This section looks at what is necessary to run a HFT strategy, from how high frequency traders route their orders to how they place their own computers for maximum speed and advantage.

Smart ordering

High frequency traders use smart order routers to take data from different market venues to ascertain where they can make a trade and where to route their own orders. Basically *smart order routers* are programs that send orders to different market venues – including both dark pool and displayed exchanges – depending on the criteria of the HFT strategy. They are mainly used to find liquidity, improve overall execution and catch rebates.

With smart ordering, orders are routed automatically to the venue with the best possible price. Some market participants believe that high frequency traders use smart routers to slow down and take a peek at their orders and then trade against those orders.

Considering the speeds that information can travel, this fear has some merit. Despite the fast speed of smart order routers, they still need to do several things and that takes time (even if it is just millionths of a second). The router needs to get the information from different market venues and then make a decision as to where to route the trade and then send the order to the venue. A risk of information leakage occurs whenever any information is sent from one place to another. As a result, some market participants recommend choosing the market venue directly without routing through a smart router.

Getting to grips with market depth: What lies beyond the sea

High frequency traders take market depth very seriously. It's what their algorithms monitor and analyse and then base their trading strategies on. What you see on the order book isn't the whole picture. Like looking at the ocean, you know that plenty is going on underneath the surface, but you can't see it.

Market depth identifies the comings and goings of the markets. Because markets move at such a frenetic pace, high frequency traders, using computer algorithms, are best equipped to analyse and trade successfully. High frequency traders send large amounts of orders to test the true depth of the market and bring out the larger volume orders.

When you look at the trading screen for any exchange and see all the bids and offers at different prices, what you're witnessing is the *depth of the market* (DOM). All the unmatched limit orders waiting to be matched make up the market depth. The more depth a market is said to have, the less of a price impact one single order will have on the underlying stock. What you see in the order book therefore tells you how *deep* a market is.

To understand how deep a market is, a trader looks at two things:

- ✔ **The number of shares:** The number of shares being offered – the more there are, the more depth there is.

- ✔ **The different prices on the order book:** The closer the different prices of the orders on both sides of the order book, the more depth there is in the market.

The spread between the bid and the offer isn't a reliable indicator of market depth. Although a market with depth will have a tight spread between the bid and the offer, it isn't necessarily an indicator of market depth.

Even the terms are often ocean related. HFT looks for *whale* orders and tries to discover the *iceberg* orders. Often plenty of hidden orders in the order book only show if certain criteria are met (refer to Chapter 8 for more detailed information). Other traders, including high frequency traders but also institutional investors with big orders, place these types of orders. The high frequency traders are particularly interested in finding these big whale orders and then trading ahead of them.

Some debate focuses on whether HFT contributes to market depth or whether it's illusory. Certainly, orders placed on the book add to the appearance of market depth. But if they're cancelled immediately whenever an order enters the market that the HFT algorithm deems as negative to its strategy then is that real market depth?

Studying the order flow to your advantage

Reading the order book used to be called *tape reading* because stock prices were printed on a ticker tape. Traders still continue to study the order flow, and watch and analyse at what price trades are executed and at what price new orders come in, or when orders are pulled.

However, with the increase of algorithmic trading and the speed at which markets move, reading the order book by eye has become next to impossible. Too much is going on for the trader to see what is really happening. The art of reading the order book hasn't changed, however; it's simply been moved to computerised analysis. The same traditional strategies are evident in these algorithms, and high frequency traders use them.

When it comes to trading on order flow, the trader is simply interested in where the market will move based on the orders that are already in the market, those that are coming into the market and those that are cancelled after a trade is executed.

The high frequency trader starts reading the order at the previous day's high and low prices, which is where orders for the new trading day are often placed. A flurry of activity and executed trades at the previous day's highs and lows can be expected. Many algorithmic trading programs have entry points and also stop losses close to these price points. High frequency traders know this, and they also trade in these areas.

Flash Boys shines light on HFT and dark pools

Partly because of the success of Michael Lewis's book *Flash Boys*, the subject of HFT and dark pools has become widely discussed. More than just a few financial insiders know about them now. Not long after the publication of *Flash Boys* Barclays bank was faced with a lawsuit regarding the operations of its own dark pool, Barclays LX, when the New York State attorney general accused Barclays of lying to its clients. Barclays soon thereafter appealed to have the case thrown out.

Soon reports followed that regulators had begun asking questions and raising suspicions about two Swiss Banks, UBS and Credit Suisse, and their own dark pools. It really has been raining down on those involved in the business of providing dark pools. All these lawsuits, fines and questions around the activities of dark pool providers make it a dangerous place to conduct trading.

Another important point that the trader watches when reading the order book is the Volume Weight Adjusted Price (VWAP) algorithm (see Chapter 7 for more on VWAP). Institutions often try to make their trades as close to the VWAP as possible. High frequency traders will try to use this information. Whenever there is even the smallest discrepancy between the VWAP and the current market price, high frequency traders will come in and move the price closer to the VWAP.

Watching the tides coming in and out: Understanding ebbs and flows

Stock markets and stocks move frequently, some faster than others, and not just when it comes to the price. The market depth and the order book can change all the time. HFT algorithms monitor these changes constantly, trying to discover in what direction the price may be moving. Even if the best bid and the best offer remain the same, changes can happen in the limit orders in the book, with some being cancelled and new ones coming in. All these movements in the order book can affect the trading models of a HFT program. For example, if several orders come into the order book to buy, it may indicate growing interest in the stock, and a HFT program will pick up on it and purchase stock in expectation of the price rising.

 You can test this yourself sometime by placing a bid or an offer some places down the order book and see what happens. Often you'll notice the order book change when your order is placed on the order book. You're best doing so with a slow moving stock. This exercise shows you that high frequency and algorithmic trading programs are working on that stock.

Predicting the Future of HFT

HFT has been a natural evolution of financial markets. Investors and traders have always looked for ways to have an edge on their competitors, and speed has always been a factor in gaining an advantage. Unfortunately, some recent negative news about dark pools in the press has put those institutions that operate HFT strategies in the sights of the regulators. (Refer to the nearby sidebar '*Flash Boys* shines light on HFT and dark pools' about where some of this press and regulation came from.)

So much public interest and increased regulatory scrutiny on the world of HFT will without doubt have an effect on the future of the industry. High frequency traders will have to adapt and adapt quickly. These sections examine how HFT and dark pools may adjust to stay viable.

Technology — staying ahead of the times

As technology continues to change, high frequency traders need to stay ahead of the curve with new technology, especially because speed is so critical to them. But there is a limit to that speed and that is the speed of light.

On one hand the high frequency traders are getting closer and closer to that limit, and on the other hand more and more investors are gaining access to tools similar to those used by high frequency traders. The technology to send information and orders at even higher speeds is coming close to reaching the wall. All the major high frequency traders will have the same speed and therefore speed will become less of a factor in the future. HFT technology then will depend more on the reliability of the infrastructure supporting the HFT and also the reliability of the algorithms that the high frequency traders use.

Markets — looking for new venues

From the beginning HFT has remained solidly an equity trading business. High frequency traders have used the abundance of different market venues, both lit and dark, to ply their trade. The competition has, however, become stronger and the profits to be made have become smaller. As a result, it's become a tough old world for those who make a living out of HFT.

In order for high frequency traders to stay competitive, they're going to look for new markets. High frequency traders will start to (and already are) trade in bonds and derivatives, and they'll branch outside of their home bases of the United States and Europe to new markets across the globe.

Keeping close Tabbs on HFT

Tabb Group, a company specialising in researching the finance industry, has found that the market share of overall trading in the United States for high frequency traders has decreased from a high of 60 per cent in 2009 to around 50 per cent in 2014. Fifty per cent is still a substantial share and will likely remain so, simply because automation is part of the modern market. As some players exit the market, new automated trading technology is being offered to new market participants. At the end of the day, though, it doesn't look like there's much growth in the industry, which explains why high frequency traders will want to look at other markets.

Market share isn't the only area that has decreased for high frequency traders. Profits have taken an even bigger hit. The Tabb Group cites that HFT revenues in the United States in 2009 were more than $7 billion, whereas in 2014 they were just over $1 billion. That's a massive drop!

You may wonder where the high frequency traders may be heading. Look out for growing economies with *liquidity poor* capital markets. Indications that markets are liquidity poor are that the trading volume is low and spreads between the bids and offers are large. High frequency traders will go to those markets, offering their services as providers of liquidity and efficient markets. That'll be their sales pitch anyway. Despite the somewhat dubious reputation of high frequency traders, many markets will be happy to have them because they'll bring about the appearance of active trading and thus give developing international market venues ammunition to promote themselves as great venues for new investors, offering them ample liquidity.

Legislation — preparing for future regulations

Because many high frequency traders tend to shy away from the public eye because of the negative press, combined with the massive public interest and confusion around what high frequency traders actually do, it's not surprising that legislators have taken notice and will continue to do so. (Chapter 6 discusses what legislators have done and plan to do to regulate dark pools.)

In order to stay one step ahead of legislators and possible new regulations, high frequency traders will have to search for new markets that aren't as regulated as the major stock markets. The industry will also consolidate as legislation wipes out many trading strategies for high frequency traders that were previously profitable, particularly those HFT strategies seen as predatory. Because HFT has been profitable for both high frequency traders and many exchanges, pro-HFT lobbyists will lobby to prevent new legislation coming into force that would inhibit HFT.

Legal actions against dark pools that have given access to high frequency traders (allowing high frequency traders to trade in their dark pools) are ongoing. If these cases ever do go to trial, they'll be setting legal precedents for the industry.

As an investor, you should stay aware of what future legislation may be coming and how it possibly could affect dark pools, automated trading and HFT. Look out for any news related to legal actions against banks or finance firms related to dark pools, automated trading and HFT. Just following the mainstream news isn't enough, though. Check the press releases, comments and guidance coming from regulators; often journalists will overlook reports that may prove pivotal to HFT. Particularly check reports that tackle how orders are routed or anything that could, when implemented, also affect high frequency traders. Most regulators can be found on social media, particularly Twitter, where they inform of their guidance and any changes planned.

Academic study — listening to the whizzes

Academics have been studying HFT for some years now, so plenty of good material is available. The majority of academic research that has come out in the past few years has been positive towards HFT. The general consensus among financial academics has been that HFT has brought cost benefits to investors in the form of tighter spreads.

This academic information can tell you and high frequency traders a lot about what to expect in the future. Pay special attention to new academic studies that question the findings of the recent years and indicate what the future holds and how legislators may take regulatory action. Start with Google Scholar to search for academic papers on dark pools and HFT. You should be able to find plenty of related academic papers there available as PDFs.

If you haven't the time or interest to read academic papers, you should at least browse through the abstract, which might have some relevant points for you and will tell you whether the subject is worth further reading. After reading the abstract, go to the sources and have a look through those. Often there may be other interesting articles to read that may not be as laborious as a full academic paper.

Chapter 11

Understanding Key High Frequency Trading Strategies

*H*igh frequency trading (HFT) is impossible without a strategy that can be programmed into a computer algorithm. This chapter looks at some of the trading strategies used by high frequency traders. Some of the strategies follow age-old trading strategies, but computer algorithms have made it possible to do them in a split second compared to what human traders what have taken much longer. Some strategies are possible only with modern technology and are unique to HFT. Some strategies are based on economic and macro news flow, whereas others are based on order book flow. Despite their differences, what they have in common is that they all use algorithmic trading programs to execute trades.

Scalping for Your Pennies

Although scalping takes place in the securities markets, the term doesn't refer to scalping the heads of traders (as much as some people would like to do that). *Scalping* in securities happens on the trading screens and the order books of the exchanges and dark pools. In terms of a HFT strategy, scalping is about making a penny here and there on a stock while playing the *bid-offer spread* back and forth, which refers to the price difference between the bid (the price at which someone in willing to buy the stock) and the offer (the price at which someone is willing to sell the stock).

The investor is the one who most of the time ends up paying the spread, selling at the bid and buying at the offer, whereas the scalper tries to act as a market maker and make the spread – selling at the offer and buying at the bid. If the scalper gets a matching order, he immediately turns around and makes a limit order on the other side of the spread to capture the spread and thus make money. It's the age-old principle of buy low and sell a little bit higher, over and over and over again. Do this enough and the pennies start turning into pounds and so on and so forth.

From this description, you can see that automated algorithmic trading is something that associates itself easily with scalping strategies because the speed allows a scalper's trading algorithm to send out and execute more trades than a human could manually send to the market. These sections examine the ins and outs of scalping.

Peering into the world of scalping

Scalping made the market what it is today. If today's market didn't have scalpers then the market wouldn't have any efficiency. The original market makers were scalpers. They got it started. They matched buyers and sellers by buying whatever it was that they were scalping and then turning around and selling it at a slightly better price to someone else. The principle for scalping in securities is simple: turn the shares over quickly at a profit.

Alternately, they agreed to sell something to someone by saying, 'Pay me now, give me a minute and I'll just pop round the corner and get it for you.' They then ran around trying to find someone to sell or lend the thing to them at a lower price. In other words, selling higher first and then buying lower. Before the days of computers this was known as *short selling*.

Scalping involves carrying risk. The person doing the scalping carries the risk on his own book. Think of an example from outside the financial markets – the ticket scalper at a giant sporting event or at a rock concert. The scalper pays for the tickets, and any profit relies on being able to sell those tickets on or before the day of the event at a higher price. The scalper is therefore said to be carrying risk.

If the tickets are for a Rolling Stones concert, more than likely the scalper is able to sell those tickets at a profit because of the massive interest in the underlying event. However, if the tickets are for a concert for an unknown act, or the local county amateur cricket match final between BumbleBoonie village and Hitherton-on-the-Wold, it's likely that tickets won't be in great demand, and the scalper probably ends up selling them at a loss.

In financial markets the trader can scalp by placing the highest bid (indication to buy) or the lowest offer (indication to sell). If the trader's order is *matched* (meaning that someone else sells or buyers from the trader), the trader immediately turns around and takes the other side of the market. For example, the market for Acme, Inc. looks like the following, and you're in the market to do a bit of scalping.

Size	Bid	Offer	Size
200	50.00	50.10	400
1,000	49.95	50.15	200
7,000	49.90	50.20	8,000
3,000	49.85	50.25	500
500	49.80	50.30	1,000

The spread is $0.10. To do a bit of scalping, you can place a bid to buy 1,000 shares at $50.01. You would be at the top of the book, like this table shows:

Size	Bid	Offer	Size
1,000	50.01	50.10	400
200	50.00	50.15	200
1,000	49.95	50.20	8,000
7,000	49.90	50.25	500
3,000	49.85	50.30	1,000

If someone comes into the market with an *at-market sell order* (an order to sell immediately at the best price available at the time, which is the best bid; read more about at market orders in Chapter 8), you immediately place an offer at the top of the book to sell your 1,000 shares at $50.09. The book then looks like this:

Size	Bid	Offer	Size
200	50.00	50.09	1,000
1,000	49.95	50.10	400
7,000	49.90	50.15	200
3,000	49.85	50.20	8,000
500	49.80	50.25	500

If someone then came into the market with an at-market buy order, you would sell the shares.

Because trades are settled at the end of the day, there's very little to stop you selling a stock before you own it. To scalp this example, you simply place both the bid and the offer at the same time.

So before your orders, the book looks like this:

Size	Bid	Offer	Size
200	50.00	50.10	400
1,000	49.95	50.15	200
7,000	49.90	50.20	8,000
3,000	49.85	50.25	500
500	49.80	50.30	1,000

After your order, the book looks like this:

Size	Bid	Offer	Size
1,000	50.01	50.09	1,000
200	50.00	50.10	400
1,000	49.95	50.15	200
7,000	49.90	50.20	8,000
3,000	49.85	50.25	500

It doesn't matter whether you get a matching order to buy or sell first. What's important is that you're in front of the queue, ready to trade both sides.

Identifying what can go wrong with scalping

Scalping sounds like a great business: sitting at the top of the book waiting for either buyers or sellers and closing your position and opening new ones, making the cash register sing like an opera singer.

Be aware: a couple things could wrong when scalping:

- **The market could move.** The price of the stock being scalped could move in a direction that leaves the trader with a loss. This can happen because of news flow that affects the price or even just a big order or orders in the stock.

- **Someone can get in front of you in the book.** Someone places an order in the market at a better price than the trader who is scalping. Because scalping is about small profits, just one order in front can wipe out a trader's profit.

If your trade gets executed and there's a big enough volume, the price may move against you, and you would be forced to take a loss on the trade.

Consider this example. The investor with the order wants to sell 2,200 shares and uses an at-market order like this:

Size	Bid	Offer	Size
1,000	50.01	50.10	400
200	50.00	50.15	200
1,000	49.95	50.20	8,000
7,000	49.90	50.25	500
3,000	49.85	50.30	1,000

On the bid side, the bid would now be $49.90, making it the last registered trade. In such a situation, it's common for the offer price to follow downward, closer to the bid price, because the spread widens while the stock is going down and other traders come in with lower offers, sensing a decline in the price and hoping to sell and then buy back at a lower price a short time later. You may find new offers coming into the market closer to the current bid. After the sale of 2,200 shares, the market could very easily look like this:

Size	Bid	Offer	Size
7,000	49.90	49.95	800
3,000	49.85	50.00	2,000
500	49.80	50.09	1,000
3,000	49.85	50.10	400
500	49.80	50.15	200

The offer is now third in line behind $49.95 and $50.00. If you placed a new offer now at the top of the book at $49.94, you would end up with a loss because you bought 1,000 shares at $50.01 with the idea to scalp them. But if you sold now at the top of the book, you would be sitting on a loss of $60 (($49.94–$50.01) × 1,000). So, as you can see, if the market moves in the wrong direction, and often it can move even with just one slightly larger order, you'll find yourself sitting on a loss.

The problem with scalping is that it's easy to jump in front of you in the order book provided that the spread is big enough. You can of course then send a new order at a new price that goes in front of the queue, but this can only go on until the spread is $0.01. After that, the ban on locked markets comes into effect. When the spread is reduced in this manner, your profit margin is greatly eroded or at worst disappears.

Scalping the automated route

In most developed markets, traditional scalping (done manually by a person) has all but died, but it's very much alive in automated form. You can easily recognise why automated trading is so conducive to scalping, and in fact most forms of algorithmic trading could be viewed as scalping. Scalping is a repetitive form of trading based on the spread of the stock, which makes it an easy strategy to program into an algorithm.

Automated trading allows for the entry of multiple orders and the changing of orders depending on how the market moves. In the same time it takes for one competent person to place an order, an algorithm will have been able to do the same thousands of time.

If you think about how simple the principle of scalping is, you can see that you don't even need a sophisticated algorithm. A basic scalping program would only require the following criteria:

- ✔ **Issue a minimum acceptable bid-offer spread:** The spread is where the profit is. The bigger the spread, the bigger the profit. The algorithm would have to have a minimum profit programmed into it, which would be the same as the minimum acceptable spread in the algorithm.

- ✔ **Place a simultaneous bid and offer:** Place both a bid and an offer at the same time.

- ✔ **Stop loss limit on open orders:** In case the market moves against the open position, define a stop loss when to exit the trade at a loss. Doing so is part of the risk management.

- ✔ **Cancel unopened orders when the minimum spread is reached:** If the spread reaches the minimum acceptable spread, the algorithm will automatically cancel all bids and offers.

- ✔ **Place a new simultaneous bid/offer on closed trades:** After a trade is *closed*, meaning there is no open position, place a new bid and offer simultaneously.

You could then attach the basic scalping program to literally hundreds of stocks and have that baby running on all of them.

Pinging to Gather Valuable Information

Pinging, often mistakenly referred to as *flash trading*, is a popular strategy for high frequency traders. (Refer to the sidebar, 'Flashing orders: The opposite of pinging', later in this chapter, for more information on flash trading). Pinging is designed to sniff out and hunt large orders. As soon as it locates large orders, it trades against them. Pinging is quite straightforward, but something that was only made possible by the emergence of HFT and algorithms. As a strategy, it's a step up in complexity from scalping.

Pinging is when an algorithm sends out a large amount of small orders (100 share lots) inside the bid-offer spread. If any of these orders is matched, the algorithm can determine whether there is a larger, hidden order in the market. Knowing that there is a large, hidden order in the market gives the opportunity for a HFT program to trade on that information for what could be a near risk-free profit.

The term *pinging* comes from submarine warfare when a submarine sends out sonar pings. When they bounce back, the submarine can figure out the presence of enemy submarines. The principle here is the same. Send out a ping and see what comes back. If you discover a big submarine then you take that baby out.

The following sections examine what happens during pinging and why pinging doesn't deserve the criticism that it sometimes faces.

Identifying what pinging does

Pinging relies on acting in milliseconds and very high speeds. It needs to be able to do four things, in this order:

1. **Detect a large trade in the market.**

   Send out several small lot orders to see whether they're matched.

2. **Confirm a large order.**

   After several small lot orders have been matched, the algorithm can deduce that there is a bigger order in the market.

3. **Trade ahead of the large order.**

   If the large order that has been detected is a buy order, for example, then the HFT algorithm will begin buying the stock.

4. **Close by trading with the large order.**

   The HFT algorithm can sell at a profit to the investor with the larger order because the HFT algorithm knows a buyer is in the market.

In other words, the whole point of a pinging strategy is to fish out a large, automated institutional order, discover the upper limit (the lower limit in the case of a sell order) of the order, drain liquidity below that limit price from the market and then sell to the institutional investor at its top limit.

Examining whether pinging is fair

Although some critics have called pinging predatory and unfair, that assessment isn't accurate. These critics may have come up with that opinion because they mistakenly confused pinging with flash orders (refer to the nearby sidebar

'Flashing orders: The opposite of pinging' in this chapter for more information on flash orders). Pinging is simply a very fast form of trying to gain market information.

Ever since trading began, traders have been trying to gain information by making assumptions, extrapolating and carrying risk, and then taking a position based on that information. *Carrying risk* means having an open position, such buying a stock and having it in the portfolio; when the stock is in the portfolio, the price is susceptible to market movements and the owner is therefore said to be carrying risk.

Looking at pinging in action

So how does a HFT program hunt out a big algorithmic order from an institution? Say that a large mutual fund is trying to buy 10,000 shares of Acme, Inc. Because it's a large order, the mutual fund's portfolio manager decides to use an algorithmic buy order that splits the purchase into smaller lots. The organisation doesn't want to move the market in one single go by planting a big buy order out there for everyone to see. It's happy to try to keep picking up shares throughout the trading day. Currently, Acme is offered at $50.50, and the highest the portfolio manager is willing to pay is $50.45. So the manager switches on the order algorithm, which starts sending in limit orders in 100 share lots.

If the trading book looks like this, the fund manager's order might be to bid 100 shares at $50.05 and see whether anything comes back (remember there may well be hidden orders in the market).

Size	*Bid*	*Offer*	*Size*
100	50.00	50.50	400
1,000	49.95	50.15	200
7,000	49.90	50.20	8,000
3,000	49.85	50.25	500
500	49.80	50.30	1,000

Say that the program sends out an immediate or cancel order (IOC) to buy 100 shares at $50.05 and nothing comes back. (An *IOC order* will immediately fill all the order it can and then cancel any remaining shares in the order that didn't get filled; refer to Chapter 8 for more information.) It then automatically sends another IOC order to buy 100 shares at $50.10. After that is executed, it then automatically sends another order to buy a further 100 shares at $50.10 and that also gets executed – great for the mutual fund manager who is buying below his limit.

Flashing orders: The opposite of pinging

Flash orders have nothing to do with men in long overcoats. Flash orders are similar to pinging, although you may often see them referred to as synonyms. You don't want to make that mistake. Think of *flash orders* as a reverse form of pinging gone stealth. *Flashing* is also a controversial form of order management, with many market participants claiming it to be unfair and manipulative. When an order comes into an exchange, prior to putting it out on the consolidated tape an exchange can flash the order to certain parties (normally, members). This flash is just a split second and allows those who see it to execute against that order.

Now when it comes to computerised trading, it really doesn't matter if the time that the order is shown is half a second or half an hour. To a fast algorithm, it makes no difference. Flashing is so contentious, because even if people privy to the flash order don't act on it, they still get valuable information regarding the intentions of other investors. They get it for just a split second and for just a split second beforehand, but that split second is more than enough time to take action. Flash orders allow high frequency traders to gain valuable information about order flow.

As a result, you can see why flash trading has its critics. There have been demands for the banning of flash orders for several years and many exchanges no longer offer them, but even though the US Securities and Exchange Commission (SEC) moved to ban flash orders in 2009, no actual ban is in effect. The use of them is completely voluntary to the exchanges.

If flash orders are used on an exchange in which you trade, and you aren't one of the parties available to see flash orders, you're pretty much guaranteed to be the one always getting the worst price possible.

Meanwhile the high frequency trader program spots this trading activity and says, 'Aha! There might be a whale in the waters.' The program then sends out a ping to test whether this is so. The high frequency trader's program then sends an IOC sell order at $50.49, and it's immediately cancelled because there's no matching order. (The maximum the mutual fund portfolio manager is willing to pay is $50.45.) The HFT program then sends out another ping to sell 100 at $50.48, which is also immediately cancelled. The program does this until it gets to $50.45 and is executed. 'Bingo!' screams the HFT algorithm. Now the program has detected the limit of what the mutual fund is willing to pay.

The HFT program now switches to buying mode, attempting to jump in front of the mutual fund by sending out buy orders that are higher than the fund manager's purchase. The mutual fund got executed at $50.10 when the HFT program detected the big order. The program then tries to gobble up liquidity all the way up to $50.45 and then sell the shares it managed to purchase to the mutual fund.

Gaming like a Casino

You know that in a casino, the house always wins. The games are set up in such a way that thanks to the laws of probability the casino always makes a profit at the cost of the gambler. High frequency traders also have been able to game the system and gain an advantage that other market participants have argued to be unfair.

High frequency traders have gamed the system in several ways. Gaming includes the use of regulatory loopholes, a lack of transparency, and collusion with brokers and exchanges to create trading situations that are advantageous to high frequency traders and disadvantageous to other market participants.

High frequency traders use some traditional forms of gaming when trading dark pools. The following sections take a closer look at the three most common.

Manipulating quotes

Quote manipulation is perhaps one of the oldest forms of gaming the market and makes use of dark pools and the Reg NMS rule on locked markets. Because of the speed required, only those individuals who have access to HFT tools can use this strategy.

Quote manipulation moves the National Best Bid and Offer (NBBO) in your favour by the use of a limit order and then executes the trade in a dark pool and then cancels the limit order. (The NBBO is a consolidated quote of all the stock exchanges in the United States showing the best bid and the best offer.) A limit order is placed in the displayed markets inside the spread so that the average price of the spread moves in the direction that the high frequency trader wants it to. After the spread has moved, the high frequency trader executes his trade in a dark pool. Because the dark pool takes the trader's price from the displayed markets, this is how the HFT trading programs game the price in a dark pool.

Quote manipulation is a basic way for you to game the price in your advantage by manipulating the NBBO. Your algorithm simply has to follow the following steps.

1. **Move the market to a favourable price by sending an opposing limit order to the displayed markets.**

   By sending a limit order inside the spread, you can move the average price of the spread in the direction you want.

2. **Send the order you want to execute to a dark pool.**

   Doing so will take the average price from the spread from the displayed market.

3. **Cancel the limit order.**

   Cancelling the limit order in the displayed market removes the order from the displayed markets and it's no longer available to trade with.

Consider this example. Say that you want to use a bit of quote manipulation, and you're selling 10,000 shares of Acme, Inc. The NBBO currently looks like this:

Size	Bid	Offer	Size
100	50.00	50.50	400

You can only sell a paltry 100 shares at $50.00. If you look at the rest of the book, you can see that you would drive the price right down to as low as $49.85 with your order of 10,000 shares as shown:

Size	Bid	Offer	Size
100	50.00	50.50	400
1,000	49.95	50.15	200
7,000	49.90	50.20	8,000
3,000	49.85	50.25	500
500	49.80	50.30	1,000

This kind of trade clearly calls for a dark pool because it's a large order, and you don't want to make a big market impact – what's more, you want to try to game the price. You can try to execute the order there. In a dark pool the order would normally be matched at the midpoint (average price) of the NBBO. In this case the price would be $50.25:

$$\frac{NBB+NBO}{2}$$
$$\frac{50.00+50.50}{2}$$

Perhaps you think you can do better. For instance, what if the National Best Bid (NBB) was higher than the current $50.00? If so, it would move the average of the NBBO up and give you a higher price.

To do so, you fire up your trusty algorithm and first send a small lot limit order to buy 100 shares at $50.45. You are now top of the book and thus your order to buy 100 shares at $50.45 is now the NBB and protected.

You may be wondering why you're sending a buy order when you want to sell. You do so because you want the mid-price of the NBBO to be as high as possible. Look at what happens now to the mid-price:

$$\frac{50.45 + 50.50}{2}$$

It's now $50.475, a full $0.225 above the midpoint prior to you sending your 100 shares buy limit order at $50.45.

You next send a sell order of 10,000 shares to the dark pool. If there is a buy order on the other side, you'll now be executed at the current mid-point of $50.475. Congratulations! You've just received $2,250 more thanks to your little limit order trick.

$50.475 \times 10,000$	504,750
$50.250 \times 10,000$	502,500
Difference	**2,250**

Don't forget, though, that your algorithm still has one thing to do. It has to cancel the limit order to buy. You need to cancel the order because you never wanted it to execute in the first place; it was simply used to move the price in your favour for the trade that you really wanted to execute. The cancellation is built into the algorithm so that it happens automatically and immediately when the trade you really wanted to execute is executed.

Taking advantage of prior knowledge: Front running

Front running is having prior knowledge of an order and acting before it. A high frequency trader can gain information about upcoming orders with

- ✔ **Flash orders:** *Flash orders* are orders that are shown for a split second to certain market participants only, the idea being that it can improve liquidity by allowing for a quicker order execution. The problem is that certain market participants gain knowledge or order flow prior to others. Refer to the sidebar 'Flashing orders: The opposite of pinging' in this chapter for more information.

- ✔ **Payment for order flow:** *Payment for order flow* is when a broker bundles up his orders and sends them to a third party for execution. Doing so adds liquidity because the receiving party trades against the orders. Often these third parties that pay for the broker's order flow are high frequency traders. Those paying for the order flow receive a large amount of information in the form of client orders. This information contains data about prices, which can have an impact on which way market prices move. For someone in that position of having market impacting data, there's a risk and temptation to use the orders and front run them. If you could see orders coming into the market before they were executed, you would gain an advantage in seeing what direction the market would be going in.

You want to sell 10,000 Acme shares. If a high frequency trader detects your order, by front running your order the trader can sell shares before you, pushing the price down and then turning around and buying your shares to cover, thus closing his own position. Because the trader sold at a higher price and bought back from you at a lower price, the trader made a profit. Chapter 12 discusses front running in greater depth and how traders can overutilise this strategy.

Part IV

Being Aware of the Risks of Dark Pools

Top five ways to avert the risks of trading in dark pools.

- ✔ **Understanding front running by high frequency traders:** High frequency traders and dark pool providers have colluded to give certain traders in dark pools an advantage.

- ✔ **Finding out the best trade execution:** Spot the dark pools where your trades are being executed at a slightly better than market price. Dark pools that execute within the spread are your friend.

- ✔ **Knowing what can go wrong:** You'll want to know all the possible causes of flash crashes to avoid being caught out in one.

- ✔ **Seeing the phantom liquidity:** Recognising phantom liquidity on the order books helps you to avoid a sudden disappearance of liquidity.

- ✔ **Bypassing the order cancellations:** High frequency traders cancel orders at a fast rate to test the market. Continuous order cancellation can be a warning of phantom liquidity and a potential of a flash crash.

Get more information on avoiding the risks of trading via dark pools at www.dummies.com/extras/darkpools.

In this part . . .

✔ Find out about the darker side of dark pools and how some dark pools have colluded with high frequency traders at the cost of their own clients so you can avoid the same fate.

✔ Discover phantom liquidity and slippage caused by high frequency traders and how you can spot it and avoid being the one paying for slippage.

✔ See the different things that commonly cause a flash crash in the markets and stay alert to the potential signs of a flash crash.

✔ Understand the causes of the famous flash crash of 2010 so you can see how all the different risks of high frequency trading can come together and cause widespread market turmoil.

Chapter 12

Jockeying Too Much for Position

- -

In This Chapter

▶ Understanding front running

▶ Cancelling orders

▶ Minimising slipping

▶ Fighting back against the algorithms

- -

*T*he equity markets consist of a giant stream of information and price data that is constantly moving and changing. News flow affects the price of stocks and so do the different bids and offers being posted on the market. Executed trades have an effect on prices, and also the orders are constantly being cancelled and revised, which moves prices one way or the other.

This perpetual stream of data all adds up to a crowded market with all the different market participants jockeying for position, trying to get the best price possible by being at the front of the order queue at just the right time. It's not just about getting a trade execution, though; the jockeying for position in the order book can also be an attempt at gathering information about how other investors and traders are valuing a stock.

This chapter shows you the different types of actions that traders and investors are involved with when trying to get the best possible price and the best possible queue position. This chapter also explains what things have an effect on the order book to move prices.

Understanding How Front Running Impacts Your Investments

Front running is nasty business. In fact, it's illegal, which sounds pretty straightforward, but it isn't. Basically, *front running* is when another market participant (for example, a broker) gets information about a trade coming into the market that will have an impact on the price and then uses that information ahead of the incoming order to profit from that order.

For example, an investor gives a broker an order to buy a certain amount of shares, but instead of buying the shares for the client, the broker buys the shares from the market, moving the price up, and then sells to the client at a slightly higher price. In this way the broker would pocket the difference. Today, a computer algorithm needs only a split second to be able to front run an order.

If you're subjected to front running then you're a victim and you end up paying for the front running in the form of higher prices when purchasing stocks or lower prices when selling stocks. Money that you needn't or shouldn't be paying goes into the front runner's pocket. Front running is an unfair practice, it distorts a fair market and it shouldn't be happening.

The following sections take a closer look at exactly what front running is and then examine it from the perspective of dark pools and HFT.

Looking at insider information

Insider information is when someone has privileged information that can affect the price of a stock and then uses that information to make money by buying or selling a stock before other market participants are made privy to the same information. Front running is a specific form of insider information.

Proving front running isn't easy

Despite the fact that nearly every country with a working stock market outlaws front running, proving that a broker, trader or high frequency algorithm is guilty of front running is difficult. The emergence of high frequency trading (HFT) algorithms and the high speed of data have made it even harder to prove because the actions happen so fast. Most of the time a client will not be able to notice anything untoward. There may also be several entities involved in front running. The one with the access to the information might not be the one executing the trade, so to prove that front running has taken place, a link must be proven between those with access to the information and those who are using the information to trade.

What once was clear black and white is now in debate. Some experts argue that HFT is legalised front running and that it happens all the time in dark pools. Then supporters of HFT argue that front running doesn't exist in dark pools; it's just that some investors have better and faster access to markets, which they claim adds value and is available to anyone who's willing or able to pay.

The big question is whether front running happens in dark pools or not. The good news: the answer is easy. Yes, front running has happened, with many documented cases.

All front running involves the use of insider information, although not all insider information is front running. Front running is the use of order flow data that will have an immediate impact on price and using that information before the order hits the market. Front running doesn't need to know why an order is being made. It's irrelevant whether the company had good quarterly results or macro-economic news flow. Front running is only about the price and the volume of an order coming into the market that will have an effect on the stock price.

For example, a broker gets an order to buy 15,000 Acme, Inc. shares at-market. If the broker immediately executed the trade, the client would get 1,000 shares at $50.10, 6,000 shares at $50.15 and 8,000 shares at $50.20. They would be an average price of $50.17 per share.

If the broker were to front run this order, the broker would buy 15,000 shares at-market and immediately put an order into the market to sell 15,000 shares at the best offer. In this case $50.24 would put the broker's order as best offer. The broker would then place the client's order to buy, and the broker would sell to the client at $50.24. The price would be $0.07 cents above what the client would have paid without the front running. For 15,000 shares, it comes to a total profit of $1,000 shares for the broker, which the client paid for.

Size	Bid	Offer	Size
200	50.00	50.10	1,000
1,000	49.90	50.15	6,000
7,000	49.85	50.20	8,000
3,000	49.85	50.25	500
500	49.80	50.30	1,000

You may be familiar with another form of insider information that isn't front running. Imagine that you're a director in a company and attending an internal meeting a week before the publication of the quarterly results. You discover that the company has beaten all sales estimates and is having an excellent quarter. You know that this information, when published, will have a positive effect on the stock price. You're now in possession of insider information. If you now act on that information by buying stock in the company before the annual results are published, you're committing the crime of using insider information.

Having priority access to information

Winning or losing in the financial markets relies on information. Market participants who have first access to the best information are the ones who end up winning. Those traders and investors who get the information in the quickest way – often because they can afford to pay for fast access to the information – can act on that information before the rest of the market, which is a highly contentious part of HFT. Some experts call this front running, whereas those market participants who defend HFT say that everyone has access to the same tools so long as they're willing to pay for them.

Having access to information earlier than some other market participants creates an opportunity and the temptation to commit front running. The need to receive quality, accurate information and the need to receive it fast has created an industry in itself. The biggest clients of the high-speed information providers are high frequency traders. The information they receive is analysed in milliseconds and then trading decisions are made based on an underlying algorithm, which immediately makes the trade.

The main way to gain access to information as quickly as possible is to get a fast data feed. Most investors rely on a consolidated feed to report prices, which means that prices from all the different stock markets are sent to one place and combined into one feed and then reported as a single data stream. Remember the ticker tape from the movies? Well, this is the updated version. In the United States, the consolidated price is known as the *Securities Information Processor feed* or the *SIP feed*.

Fast access to stock information relies on *co-location* – a term used to describe placing a firm's own servers physically as close as possible to the servers of the exchanges. Brokers, banks and high frequency traders are willing to pay big money to achieve this. Using co-location price information leaves the exchange to the firm at autobahn speeds, whereas that same information travelling to the consolidated feed takes the slower road, stopping off at the point at which prices are consolidated before being sent out as one feed. Refer to Chapter 10 for more discussion on the basics of co-location and why it's important.

Co-location services provide a great revenue generator for stock exchanges that face increased competition from dark pools for trading volume and also face increased pressure on fees. So, basically, high frequency traders, banks and brokers pay enough money, and they get to travel faster than others in the market, which gives them an obvious advantage. Well, yes, but in the US market it gets a little bit more complicated.

Remember the Securities Information Processor (SIP) newsfeed, the US consolidated price feed? Well, providing a direct data feed to a subscriber faster than providing that information to the SIP feed is prohibited in the United States. The price information from an exchange must therefore arrive at the direct feed subscriber and the SIP processor at the same time.

So how does paying for a direct feed give high frequency traders an advantage if they receive the information at the same time as the SIP? Well, the problem lies with the SIP. Think of the problem as a bottleneck in a traffic jam. All orders arriving in the SIP feed receive a new time stamp when they're forwarded on to the consolidated feed. Because information can move as fast as 0.0001 seconds, these tiny increments make things very difficult indeed. If the clock in one exchange is off by a few milliseconds from the clock of the SIP feed, it's impossible to know and compare the time stamp reliably with that of the data feed.

As a result, the high frequency traders, banks and brokers with the financial capabilities are willing to pay big money to be guaranteed an accurate information feed.

Feeding the news data quickly

Financial news releases, particularly economic indicators, profit warnings and corporate results, can have an immediate and sudden impact on the markets and stocks that the data relates to. This is especially evident when a news release differs from market expectations or comes as a surprise to markets. Receiving this information first and being able to act on it before others is a form of front running and can be very profitable.

News service providers also offer, for those who can pay of course, slightly faster access to the news than others. They might actually sell the service so that a major news report is released to certain subscribers a few milliseconds faster than the actual market.

A few milliseconds may as well be a few weeks with modern technology. Selling access to potential market impacting news prior to its release to the whole market is a controversial system. For a fair market to operate, price impacting news should be available to all at the same time. This is why regulators may well come up with rules and procedures to limit any practice seen as giving a head-start to those market participants who pay for first access to news data.

These news feeds are commonly referred to as *low-latency news services*. The news service providers set the news up in such a way that their clients (high frequency traders) are able to use their high frequency algorithms to make trading decisions based on the released news. The news release is structured so that a trader or investor's algorithm can read the news, pick out keywords and numbers, make an analysis and come up with a trading decision.

Leaking news

News reports can be leaked, and some evidence indicates that it actually happens. Leaked news is valuable information because news and data will affect the markets. This has been particularly evident when the news release has been contrary to the general consensus because such news reports nearly always move prices.

Having access to leaked news information offers the possibility to front run because the information isn't yet in the public domain. A trader with access to leaked information can make an analysis of the price impact of the news and then make a trade based on the analysis.

There are two types of leakage and they are very different from each other:

- **Happens minutes prior to the official release:** The price movements that happen minutes prior to the official release occur during what is known as a lock-up time. The *lock-up time* refers to the period prior to official release when approved news reporters are given the information so that they can file their news story to be released at exactly the same time as the report is released.

- **Happens almost immediately (within nanoseconds now) upon the release:** The price movements that happen within nanoseconds of the official release may at first appear to be only relevant to superfast computers that are able to make decisions quickly. Although this is true in part, there's an interesting little conundrum at play. Information still takes time to travel from one place to another, but sometimes prices have moved faster than the information could possibly travel – interesting to say the least.

These sections examine these two forms in greater depth to help you understand how they can influence front running.

Locking up the news

Organisations release their data and reports to reporters before releasing the reports to the public so that reporters have time to read the reports or statistics and then prepare their own news stories. Doing so makes the news more reader friendly and improves the quality of the reporting. They normally do so about 10 to 30 minutes prior to the public release of the news, which is called the *lock-up time.*

Different organisations have differing rules for their lock-up procedures. A common method is to have the reporters convene in one room, ban the use of mobile phones and disconnect the Internet.

Having access to the information before it's released is valuable. After all, if the news report differs from the consensus forecasts, it can move markets suddenly, so there's a high demand for this information. Where financial gain can be had there's the temptation for nefarious actions.

Study shows the good and bad of leaking news

Studies have provided evidence that news leakage does happen. In 2014 a team of academics from the Singapore Management University found evidence that in some cases prices do move during the lock-up period prior to the official release. The study, called 'Can information be locked-up? Informed trading ahead of macro-news announcements', by Gennaro Bernile, Jianfeng Hu and Yuehua Tang, analysed government agencies' economic data releases and market movements during the lock-up period. The data is compelling and covers the period from 1997 to 2013.

The data analysed included the following:

✔ Announcement of the Federal funds target rate from the Fed

✔ Nonfarm payrolls

✔ Consumer Price Index (CPI) from the US Department of Labor

✔ Gross domestic product (GDP) by the Bureau of Economic Analysis

The study compared movements in the E-Mini futures contract, which is a liquid and commonly used futures contract based on the S&P 500 index. They found that when it came to the Fed's announcement, the price of the E-Mini did in fact move during the lock-up period, when the released news differed from the consensus.

'Consistent with information leakage, we find robust evidence of informed trading during lockup periods ahead of the Federal Open Market Committee (FOMC) monetary policy announcements.'

What that means in plain English is that the researchers have a smoking gun that shows someone who knew about the information traded or leaked information to someone who traded on that information. They gave two figures as proof of this. First, there was an order imbalance of around 9 per cent, which meant that there was a build-up of orders on the side of the order book where the market would move when the news was to be released. For example, if the news was a positive surprise, buy orders built up in the book ahead of the release. The second figure the study mentioned was a move of 0.2 per cent in the E-Mini during the lock-up period. It doesn't seem like much, but the E-Mini is highly liquid and even small movements can add up to big numbers.

However, the study didn't find evidence that CPI or GDP suffered from information leakage. So it seems it's just the Federal Reserve that has a problem with this issue.

Reporters can sometimes be responsible for leakage, or sometimes someone with the information trades during the lock-up period with the intention of putting the blame on the reporters. Whatever the reason, as an investor you should avoid trading in markets affected by upcoming economic data that has a history of information leakage.

Government agencies regularly release reports, statistics and economic indicators to reporters that can have an effect on financial markets. Some of the most followed reports include the following:

- **The Federal Reserve (FOMC):** The Federal Reserve (Fed) is responsible for the setting of US interest rates. Changes in US interest rates can have an effect on most global markets, equities, bonds and currencies. Whenever the Fed does something, particularly if it's a move that differs from consensus estimates, it's an across-the-market-affecting event.

- **Nonfarm payrolls:** This is an important monthly economic indicator for the United States. Nonfarm payrolls report the current situation of the US employment market. Traders, investors and economists then use the information to analyse and predict the direction of the US economy. The indicator is important because it can have an effect on equity, bond and currency markets across the globe.

- **Gross domestic product (GDP):** The Bureau of Economic Analysis (BEA) releases this economic indicator. The indicator gives an overall view of the US economy, and traders and investors closely follow it.

For more information about different economic indicators that may be important to you, check out *Economic Indicators For Dummies* by Michael Griffis (John Wiley & Sons, Inc.).

Be on the lookout during this period for changes in the order book. High frequency traders will often attempt to read orders coming into the book during the trading lock-up, trying to ascertain where the market might move when the news is released.

On release

News leaks also happen immediately upon the release – within nanoseconds – and it's a winner takes all race. Those who are the quickest to execute their trades are the winners, and any news that has a price effect will be priced in immediately that the news is released.

When a trader has access to direct news feeds, which have been structured in a manner that make them easy for trading algorithms to analyse and make trading decisions on, there is no chance for any investor or trader who operates manually to act upon that news. You can find a real life example of this in the nearby sidebar 'Leaking news on release'.

To protect yourself, don't try to trade around economic data releases. The moves are so fast and the competition to be first is so fierce that the chances for success, even for those with co-location and fast algorithmic programming, are slight. If you're an individual private investor then your chances are non-existent. You're far better off analysing the news release in your own time, making a decision and only then entering a trade. By this time any HFT effects will have been priced into the underlying market.

Pay attention to the order book during the lock-up period. Any imbalances can be an indicator as to the direction of the move when the news data is eventually released.

Leaking news on release

The controversy around news releases and HFT started in 2013 when market experts discovered that markets in different geographical positions reacted to a Fed announcement at exactly the same time. In this case the geographical positions in question were Washington, D.C., where the news is released, and New York and Chicago, where trading in instruments affected by the release is conducted.

This may not appear so strange at first, but if you look at it from a high frequency point of view it's significant. The news is released in Washington, D.C., and for the information to reach New York and Chicago takes a few milliseconds. The fastest it could possibly go is the speed of light, which can travel at about 186 miles per millisecond. Travelling at the speed of light puts three milliseconds of time between Washington, D.C., and Chicago and a little over a millisecond between New York and Washington, D.C.

This doesn't take into account how fast the information actually moves. Nor does it take into account the computation needed to analyse the news and come up with a trading decision and send an order to market.

The fact is that there is a time difference, and if the news is released in Washington, D.C. then trading on the news release could not happen at the same time. So what did happen?

Trading really did begin in both New York and Chicago at exactly the same time that the news from Washington, D.C., was released. How is this possible? The explanation is rather simple. The reports had to be sent to New York and Chicago prior to the release.

This situation was first highlighted by a Chicago based company called Nanex, which analyses market data down to the millisecond. Its findings were then disputed by a high frequency trading firm called Virtu Financial.

What added to the confusion was that neither the Fed nor some of the news agencies present during the embargo were willing to comment on whether they had indeed downloaded their reports to different geographical locations during the embargo.

It's likely then that the information was sent and loaded onto computer servers at the exchange and released at exactly the same time. After investigation the Futures Industry Association (FIA) released a statement theorising that because news agencies have computer servers in several locations and there is no ban on uploading news releases to their servers, the fact that information was released at the same time in several locations should've been expected.

Examining Order Cancellations

This number may surprise you: according to the Securities and Exchanges Commission 97 per cent of all orders sent to the US stock exchanges are cancelled. That's an awful lot of cancellations. Traders are making a lot of incorrect inputs, or something else is going on.

An *order cancellation* is the sending of an order to the market and then removing it. With an algorithm, it's possible to repeat this process at a constant rate and in milliseconds. The large amount of order cancellations is caused by algorithms constantly updating their prices and sending orders based on the cancellations of other traders and also new orders coming in.

These sections examine what else is going on in terms of jockeying for position by high frequency traders, why they constantly revise their orders and why sometimes they send a large amount of orders into the market in a very short amount of time.

Gathering information

Information gathering happens when high frequency traders send out orders to try to find big orders lurking in the markets so that they can decide on the possible direction of a stock's price movement.

One way of finding out whether large orders are in the market is to send smaller baby orders into the market and see whether any of them are executed. If an order isn't filled then it can be cancelled and a new order sent in at a new price. If, for example, a high frequency trader sends an order into a dark pool to sell 100 shares at the mid-price and the order gets executed then the trader can send in another similar order. If that new order is also executed, the trader can deduce that a large buy order is in the pool. The trader can then use this information to start purchasing the stocks and then sell them in the pool to the large order.

By sending out small orders at a rapid rate, an HFT program hopes to find a price point at which hidden orders will be executed. After it believes it has found such an order, the program can then trade against the order to make money. The investors most affected by this action are institutional investors with large orders. If you're trying to execute a large order then you're in danger of either paying a higher price than necessary or getting a lower price than you deserve because a high frequency trader finds your order and trades against it.

Stuffing quotes

Quote stuffing is a nefarious action. Some argue that it doesn't exist, but there is evidence that it does happen. *Quote stuffing* happens when a firm sends out a massive amount of buy and sell orders and immediately cancels them. Doing so can overload the exchange computers and slow down the execution of trading. Some firms have been fined specifically for quote stuffing.

Quote stuffing creates opportunities for high frequency traders. Many stocks are correlated and indices are formed out of baskets of stocks. By slowing down a particular stock, a HFT program can in theory trade a correlated stock or index, knowing that after the backlog is removed, the price will revert to normal.

Quote stuffing causes a decrease in liquidity and an increase in volatility. Both of these combine to increase the cost of trading. If a trader is able to manipulate the liquidity of a stock and its volatility then it gives that trader profitable trading possibilities.

Playing games

Gaming is another controversial tactic used in conjunction with dark pools. *Gaming* means the manipulation of the NBBO, by moving the spread in the displayed markets by placing an order within the spread and then executing a trade in a dark pool and cancelling the order that was placed in the displayed market. Doing so affects the whole jockeying for position because the order in the displayed markets was never intended to be executed. It was there only to move the NBBO before it would be cancelled. You can read more about gaming in the Chapter 11.

Identifying the Impact of Slippage

Slippage is common in trading. In fact, it's actually inevitable and always has been. *Slippage*, which is more formally referred to as *implementation shortfall*, basically means the difference between what you want to pay and what you eventually end up paying.

Slippage is of great concern to large, institutional investors. If you're investing a lot of money and doing it frequently, those few cents of price difference start to really add up. Slippage is in effect a form of commission and should be calculated as part of trading costs.

When other market participants detect a large order in the market, for example a large buy order, they will inevitably cancel their offers, which will *slip* the offer side prices on the book upward. At the same time bids will start coming into the order book, trying to buy ahead of the large order. This cancelling of offers and posting of new, higher bids will slip the stock's price upward.

High frequency traders are often on the other side of a trade that causes slippage. Their strategies are designed to instigate slippage, and as a result make money from the resulting move. The most common situation is when a HFT program believes that it has found a larger order. In the case of a buy order, the program uses its speed to start buying shares on the market so that it can sell them back to the larger buyer at a higher price. The knowledge that there is a larger order hiding in the market causes slippage in the price, and the larger order will have to pay a higher price than it originally intended.

Consider this example of slippage. Say that you want to buy 1,000 shares of Acme, Inc. and you're willing to buy them at the going market rate. You look at the bid and the offer and see that the offer is $50.10 for 1,000 shares as the following shows; exactly the amount you want to buy. You decide that's fine and hit the buy button, but just a split second before you, someone else has also pressed the buy button at-market for 1,200 shares.

Size	Bid	Offer	Size
200	50.09	50.10	1,000
1,000	49.95	50.15	200
7,000	49.90	50.20	8,000

That trader's order hits the market faster than yours, thanks to *price time priority*, which indicates the orders be executed first based on price and then according to which order came arrived on the book first (refer to Chapter 3 for more information on this). So the trader gets 1,000 shares of her order at $50.10 and the remaining 200 shares at $50.15. You, on the other hand, were expecting to pay only $50.10 and end up actually paying $50.20 – 10 cents more per share than you originally expected. You have just been on the receiving end of slippage – or, if you want to sound fancy, you can say implementation shortfall.

Knowing What You Can Do to Mitigate These Risks

Assuming that you can't afford co-location services and don't have a degree in advance mathematics, you can still do a few things to reduce the risk of having to pay for the profits of high frequency traders.

Do the following to reduce your risks:

✔ **Play detective.** The most important thing you can do is gather as much information as possible from your broker regarding how she routes your orders. Check to see how much of the trades are internalised and whether your broker uses dark pools. If your broker does use dark pools, find out which ones she uses and read up on those specific pools. Refer to Chapter 2 for how you can work closely with your broker.

✔ **Discover what types of special orders are used.** For instance, check to see whether the broker changes limit orders or market orders to other types of special orders. Ask plenty of questions in writing and receive answers in writing. Some specific questions to ask include

- Do you use special order types?

- Can you supply me with a list of special order types you use?

- Are my orders at any point changed by you to a specific special order type?

✔ **Provide clear, upfront directions in writing.** Put in writing any specific directions about the ways that you want your orders processed and what you don't want done. Giving written directions requires that you're knowledgeable about the specific exchanges and dark pools being used and what kind of orders they have.

Unfortunately, being certain that your orders are being handled the way you want them to be handled can be difficult. That's why expressing your questions and concerns in writing and insisting on getting your answers in writing are important. Chapter 2 can offer some helpful advice about communicating with your broker.

✔ **Choose a provider that offers algorithmic and trading tools.** More brokers now offer these tools with fast data feeds to clients. The minimum balance for such accounts is becoming smaller, so you need to shop around. Using these services requires a lot of study on your part, though. You need to know the ins and outs of the various market places and you need to know the special order types. For more specific advice about what to ask your prospective broker, check out Chapter 15.

✔ **Trade with a large index ETF.** Trading with a large exchange traded fund (ETF) may not be as exciting, but you'll be riding the wave with the big boys; going with a major ETF can be safer than trading individual stocks. ETFs are a big part of high frequency traders' strategies, and by jumping on the bandwagon you'll be able to be in sync with them. Trading with a large ETF is a passive way of investing and doesn't involve trading actively.

Choose a large index and a liquid ETF. Doing so gives you the smallest possible spread between the bid and offer and also the necessary liquidity to get in and out at a good price. Simply collect a list of the ETFs available for the index you want to invest in and look at their average daily trading volume and the spread that they trade at during the market opening hours. Choose the one with the largest volume and the smallest spread.

Market crashes do occur, and then ETFs are the most vulnerable because they track the whole market and therefore bear the brunt of all the market turmoil. To better understand market crashes, refer to Chapter 13.

The options for you as an investor to defend yourself against being the prey of high frequency traders are limited. It's the regulators' job to do that, and thankfully there have been advances in regulation. As the debate around HFT and dark pools has entered the public sphere, regulators are working to come up with regulation that meets the demands of today's markets. Refer to Chapter 6 for more information about how legislators have worked to regulate markets.

Chapter 13

The Ins and Outs of Flash Crashes

....

In This Chapter

▶ Understanding how flash crashes happen

▶ Looking closer at the flash crash of 2010

▶ Analysing a flash crash

....

Markets have become faster and faster during the past decade and so have market crashes. Crashes in individual stocks, indices and whole exchanges can happen so fast that they're over in a flash, which is where the term *flash crash* comes from. These crashes can happen in a matter of minutes, seconds or even milliseconds, faster than your eye can spot them. *Flash crashes* are a sudden drop in the price of a stock or index. Often the cause of these crashes is attributed to algorithms, either going wrong because of faulty computer programming, or because of human error.

You certainly don't want to be on the receiving end when a flash crash happens, so having a handle on what they are and how they happen is imperative for you. This chapter explains how flash crashes occur. I focus on how the greatest flash crash of all happened in 2010. You can also find out how you can analyse a flash crash after it has happened so you can avoid getting caught up in one in the future.

Grasping How Flash Crashes Happen

A *flash crash* is simply a big, sudden drop in the value of a stock or an index. When it comes to individual stocks, flash crashes fortunately aren't that uncommon. When they do identify them, you need to know how they occurred. A few common reasons for flash crashes include the following:

- ✔ News flow
- ✔ Human error
- ✔ Computer error

The following sections explain these three reasons in greater depth so that you can see who the main culprits are behind flash crashes.

Blaming the news flow

When negative news reports come out concerning a particular stock, for example a profit warning, the stock's price can drop immediately by a significant amount. With the sheer amount of different stocks to invest in, these news-related events are part of the day-to-day of your investing experience. The price of a stock is the market's valuation of a company's overall value at that particular moment in time.

Any news regarding a specific stock can have an effect on the success (or not) of a company, and the price of a stock will readjust to the news. For that reason news flow can kick off a flash crash because the news can create a knock-on effect as algorithms detect the change in price and activity in the order book and withdraw orders, thus erasing the bid side in the order book.

However, although the sudden drop in the price of a stock can be called a flash crash, keep in mind that when the media refers to a *flash crash*, it probably doesn't mean this particular scenario. Most of the time when you hear the term it's in reference to a faulty computer program or human error unrelated to the fundamental of the underlying stock.

Holding humans responsible

Mistakes happen and they can happen to anyone (maybe not for those with slender fingers, though). Despite the growing use of algorithmic programs for trading, plenty of institutions and investors still input orders manually. Manual input means that making mistakes isn't unusual. The most common form of mistake is simply inputting the wrong amount of stock or the wrong price. Often these types of mistakes are referred to as *fat-finger orders* because of an imaginary trader with fingers so fat that he struggles to press his digits on a keyboard one at a time.

What if you intend to buy 10,000 shares of XYZ, but by accident you lean on the 1 and the 2 digits simultaneously and a little too long on the 0, and then you press enter before noticing your mistake? Your order of 10,000 shares now turns into an order of 2,100,000 shares. That's a big difference.

This example is the trading equivalent of a major typo, and as you well know, typos happen to everyone. For someone placing trades throughout the day these mistakes can easily happen. Normally, there are warnings and safeguards in systems that highlight orders that appear to be incorrect, but no system is perfect and fat-finger orders are still part of the trading landscape and can be a possible trigger for a flash crash.

Other types of human error can occur in other areas as well. When it comes to algorithmic trading programs, some are designed specifically for placing large orders in the market. The aim of these programs is to hide the large volume of the order by inputting the large order in smaller *baby* lots so as not to affect the market price. This practice is common with institutions that trade in large amount of shares.

Computer programmers design algorithmic trading programs; however, portfolio managers and traders (who aren't computer programmers) use them and sometimes those who design the program and those who design the trading strategy don't quite understand what it is that each other wants from the trading program. Several possible factors have to be taken into account when choosing how an order is placed into the market. Some of the important ones are as follows:

- ✔ Total size of order
- ✔ How the order is broken down
- ✔ A set limit price
- ✔ The kind of order to use
- ✔ Where the order is routed
- ✔ How long the order is in place

Omitting or choosing the wrong type of input to any of the above parameters can have unintended consequences and cause what's called a *knock-on effect*, resulting in a flash crash.

Due to the choice and complexity of special order types available today (you can read more about them in Chapter 9), the person inputting the order into the market may not be completely knowledgeable as to how the order interacts in the market. For instance, an error such as replenishing the baby orders too quickly can have a sudden impact on the share price, which can contribute to a flash crash.

Computer programming loops

Despite the rigorous testing and planning of computer programs, things can and do go wrong. Computer errors can cause an array of problems, sometimes culminating in a flash crash.

One of the most feared things for any trading programmer is a glitch in an algorithm that causes the program to trade at a loss over and over again in milliseconds, causing significant losses. A testing environment for a computer program isn't the same as the real market. A faulty program, when let loose on the markets, may interact with the market in an unintended way.

For example, a company called Knight Capital, a large market maker, nearly went bankrupt when its new trading algorithm had a glitch that caused losses of more than $400 million in just a matter of minutes. The company was trying a new market-making algorithm that traded in more than 100 stocks, sending out thousands of orders a second.

These kinds of losses-making trading loops can occur for a couple of reasons:

✔ **The programming has a simple omission.** The person or people responsible for planning the trading strategy haven't informed those responsible for building the trading program with enough detail of the strategy.

✔ **Testing with historical data doesn't take into account new and unusual market conditions.** The market changes, and although history has a tendency to repeat itself, it doesn't do so in exactly the same way. New events such as natural disasters, corporate results surprises and regulatory changes can all have an unexpected effect, which can cause an algorithm to trade in unintended ways.

Without a working automated kill switch in the trading program and with several thousand trades being sent out in milliseconds, any human intervention after the problem is noticed is probably too late. The losses are likely to be substantial.

Eyeing How Flash Crashes Spook the Whole Market

The speed at which a flash crash occurs can have serious repercussions, particularly if it lasts several minutes. That's enough for slower market participants who aren't using superfast technology to see the markets or the shares they're trading in take a dive. As a result, these slower traders panic and send sell orders to the market, thus adding to the crash's severity.

In general, markets can react to negative news without too many problems. Whatever underlying sector or stock the news affects has a habit of simply re-evaluating the news and then moving the price of the stock or the market to take into account the effect of the news. Although this idea sounds simple, the markets have trouble pricing the uncertainty.

The speed at which flash crashes happen and the lack of any clear reason at the time scares markets more than a negative jolt of news. A flash crash also can have a knock-on effect because other investors react to a flash crash. What is happening to one share can quickly spread to other stocks in the same sector, across whole exchanges and even infect other asset classes.

Flash crashes draining liquidity

Flash crashes cause confusion, which has a tendency to make investors sell or stop trading by pulling out of the market. These two things tend to happen in unison. *Draining liquidity* is when orders are cancelled without renewing them, and those posting orders are only doing so on one side of the order book – in the case of a flash crash, posting them only on the offer side. As a result, the market has less volume on offer to trade with and even less on the buy-side to absorb the inevitable selling that happens.

As sell orders come into the market, the trading book on the bid (buy-side) becomes smaller. Thus even small orders are able to move the price of the stock downward. This kind of liquidity drain can happen in an instant as computer algorithms detect an abnormal move and withdraw from the market; or jump onto the offer (sell-side) of the order book; or worse yet begin *hitting the bid*, which means sending out at-market sell orders, when detecting a downward trend.

Going from a lively market to a ghost town: Volume isn't relevant

Trading volume isn't an indication of liquidity. In flash crashes you'll often see an increase in volume, but that increase doesn't mean more liquidity, which sounds confusing, but in fact it's not.

Think of it like a game of hot potato. For a market to have liquidity you don't just need traders (you need those too) but also different types of market participants with different goals; you need net buyers and net sellers. By *net buyers* or *sellers*, I mean investors who are taking a position, something that lasts for longer than a millisecond or two, even overnight or, good heavens, a week or more!

In a flash crash only a few participants are left in the market as real liquidity drains but trading volume may well rise. The increased volume combined with a decrease in actual market participants is due to the computer algorithms going back and forth between each other, buying and selling stocks. Despite the rise in volume, only a few players are left in the market, trading between themselves.

Viewed from this perspective the liquidity isn't real. The market is in reality a ghost town, but the volumes tell you a completely different, and wrong, story.

Examining the Greatest Flash Crash of All Time

The greatest flash crash of all time happened on 6 May 2010, when several different but interlinked markets fell several percentage points in just a matter of minutes, only to quickly recover. The New York Stock Exchange (NYSE) was forced to break several thousand trades as erroneous because the prices were so far away from anything resembling fair value. *Breaking* a trade means to cancel and to make null and void a trade that has already been executed.

The NYSE's reason for breaking so many trades was that so many of the trades had been executed at prices that were clearly far away from a realistic and fair value of the underlying stock. The movements in stocks were so big that some stocks ended up being traded at just a cent while others exchanged owners at $100,000.

It was one of the first times that the risks of automated trading and high frequency traders were brought into the public eye. Knowing the causes and effects of the great flash crash of 2010 helps you see the risks as well as understand how high frequency trading (HFT) and automated trading interact with the markets.

The flash crash of 2010, although not completely new as a phenomenon, was on such an unseen scale that all kinds of different theories cropped up, and the Securities and Exchanges Commission (SEC) even conducted a thorough investigation of the causes and later published its findings. This report didn't convince all market participants, though, and differing theories still exist as to the real causes.

In these sections, I examine the different triggers that started the flash crash and also look at the possible causes of the flash crash.

The perfect storm triggered

Just like an air crash, seldom does a single thing cause a flash crash, although a trigger may set things in motion. Often a combination of several things going wrong or a succession of events that becomes too much for the market to handle cause a crash.

In hindsight, on 6 May 2010 elements were in place for a perfect market storm. The stock markets were already trading a few percentage points lower than the previous day, but then at 2:42 p.m. the Dow Jones Industrial Average (a benchmark of 30 large US listed stocks) began to fall, and within five minutes it had dropped approximately 6 per cent, only to regain those losses just a few minutes after.

The drop was one of the biggest falls in a single day in the history of the Dow Jones Index, and the speed was something that had seldom been seen before. At first, market observers were at a loss to comprehend what had happened and many blamed a computer glitch, which is a commonly used catchall phrase to describe the cause of a flash crash in a stock or index before the real cause is discovered. You should always be wary when you hear that term and investigate further.

Theorising about the causes

Pundits initially analysed the crash and determined that a computer glitch was the cause. After further analysis, other theories for the cause included the following:

- ✔ **Hackers:** Computer hackers were suspected to have hacked into exchange servers and manipulated the order books in the exchange.

- ✔ **Terrorist hackers:** Even Al-Qaeda terrorists were blamed. People accused them of hacking into the markets to cause an economic collapse and damage the stability of the United States.

- ✔ **High frequency traders:** Large amounts of HFT orders caused a slow-down in the market's ability to match trades, causing havoc, and so brought about the flash crash.

- ✔ **A fat-finger order or other human error:** Some theories suggested that a fat-finger order had added a few extra zeroes to an order, thus causing a panic run out of the door by investors. Refer to the earlier section 'Holding humans responsible' for more information how human error could cause a crash.

- ✔ **Rogue algorithms:** Algorithms acting in a way not planned to when programmed caused a flurry of orders that set off the flash crash.

No evidence of these types of conspiracies has been found and the general consensus is that it was a combination of things and had nothing to do with hackers or terrorists.

The SEC conducted its own investigation and published a report. Other respected market observers also came out with their own theories backed by data. Although the theories still differ somewhat, they're unified in the belief that the problems were a combination of issues coming together at the same time.

The SEC Speaks: The Official Version of the 2010 Flash Crash

The SEC took nearly five months to finish its official analysis into the causes of the flash crash of 6 May 2010. Many market participants immediately called into question the reliability of the study, but it remains the only official version of the day's events.

The SEC faced criticism for lacking the up-to-date resources, technology and know-how to be able to understand, let alone conduct a study into the causes of a modern flash crash. As proof of these shortfalls, critics pointed out the length of time that it took the SEC to study what were just a few minutes of market action. In some respects this criticism is unfair because the amount of data that had to be sifted through for that time was vast and involved several market venues. It remains an important study, and you need to know the basics of the finding to fully understand the modern market place.

These sections provide you with an overview of what the approximately 100-page SEC study reported. You can find the complete study by visiting the SEC website at www.sec.gov/news/studies/2010/marketevents-report.pdf.

Noting the market's appearance

The state of the overall global markets is an important factor in what happened in the flash crash of 2010, and the SEC points out this factor in its study. Overall uncertainty in the global markets was increasing prior to the flash crash. Europe was in the midst of a sovereign debt crisis, which in its simplest form meant that their governments had borrowed more than they could pay back. Countries such as Greece, Spain and Portugal were facing increased borrowing costs, and the cost of insuring against default on European sovereign debt had climbed. Investors feared that the problems would have a knock-on effect on the world economy, which remained fragile after the Credit Crunch and the fall of Lehman Brothers bank in 2008.

Because of the prevailing fears for the European economy, volatility started to increase, as could be seen in a rise in the VIX index (Chicago Board Options Exchange Market Volatility Index), which is sometimes referred to as the *fear index*. Gold prices also increased, because many investors often view gold as a secure investment in times of economic uncertainty.

Basically, the market was a little scared as trading started on 6 May. As a result, as soon as the US markets opened, they started heading downwards.

Although these events have little to do with HFT, you need to be aware of the background because the economic events effecting the market sentiment at the time lay the backdrop that made circumstances possible for a flash crash – at least according to the SEC.

Interconnecting markets

As markets have become more global and faster, correlations between different market venues and different types of asset classes have grown. In other words, movement in one market inevitably causes a change in another.

You always need to keep this in mind when following HFT and dark pools: nothing happens in a vacuum on its own. Individual stocks are connected to indices and stock movements are related to movements in different types of bond and derivative markets.

ETFs

Exchange trade funds (ETFs) are similar to mutual funds. However, they have lower trading costs because they aren't actively managed. They simply follow an underlying index. Whereas traditional mutual funds are normally traded only once a day, ETFs are traded on an exchange (as the name implies), so whenever an exchange venue is open, the fund can be traded in real time.

ETFs are an integral part of HFT because high frequency traders employ strategies that buy and sell an index ETF and the underlying stocks within the index, trying to catch small difference in price. (Refer to Chapter 11 for some of these strategies.)

One of the most popular ETFs is an ETF known as SPY, which tracks the S&P 500 index. It's the biggest ETF in the world and very popular with traders because of its liquidity. The S&P 500 index was at the heart of events during the 2010 flash crash.

Derivatives

Derivatives are popular for hedging investments. Like the name implies, they derive their value from something else. In the case of the 2010 flash crash, the derivatives mentioned in the SEC report derived their value from the S&P 500 index.

Typically, the movements in the price of a derivative are much larger than the underlying due to leverage. Some investors may take an opposite position in a derivative of an existing investment, so that they can protect against losses. Hedge funds aren't the only ones who are interested in derivatives; traders – particularly high frequency traders – like derivatives also.

As part of the global market, derivatives, especially those tracking large benchmarks such as the S&P 500, are popular and very liquid. The SEC's study concentrated on movements in the E-Mini S&P 500 contract, which is traded on the Chicago Mercantile Exchange and is the world's most popular equity index futures contract.

The SEC's study focused on one particularly large order of 75,000 contracts in the E-Mini by one investor.

Individual stocks

Most of the action in the SEC's 2010 flash crash report centred on the S&P 500 stock index, which means that inevitably individual stocks were also involved. Some HFT algorithms look for discrepancies between the index and the stocks that make up that index. When such a situation is spotted, they can either buy or sell the stock or index and exit the position as soon as the index or stock normalises, thus leaving them with a profit.

As the crash happened, there were wild swings in individual stocks with some going as low as $0.01 and some going as high as $100,000 before quickly recovering again to normal levels. The NYSE was forced to cancel some of these trades on account of them being so unrealistic.

Identifying the participants

Knowing which players were involved with the flash crash of 2010 can also perhaps explain what caused it. These sections introduce you to them.

Equity market makers

Equity market makers have a responsibility to provide an orderly market. In the strictest sense of the name, market makers have an obligation to quote both sides of the market, which means they have to provide both a bid and an offer for a stock. This explains one of the reasons that during the 2010 flash crash some stocks were traded at $0.01. They were known as *stub quotes*, which market makers place in the market to fulfil their quoting requirements without having any intention of getting them filled.

The SEC report, however, decided to classify market makers a little differently when it came to the E-Mini contract. In addition to the actual registered market makers, the report included those market participants who traded a significant amount of contracts inside a single trading day. In the study, market makers for the E-Mini were classified as those 'who follow a strategy of buying and selling a large number of contracts, but hold a relatively low level of inventory'.

You can refer to Chapter 5 for more basic information about what market makers are and what they do.

Investors

Investors who take on longer-term positions and hold them, or use derivatives to hedge their positions, were also present in the market and were a factor in the day's events. They're the more traditional investors who take on so-called *net positions*, which means that they hold on to the stocks they purchase with a longer-term horizon.

Traditional investors are more important to the liquidity of a market than many high frequency traders give them credit for. In fact, think of them as a foundation for the market. If they aren't present in the market then only traders are left and the process of discovering the correct value of an asset is compromised. Traders who are just trading in and out of an asset, like high frequency traders, don't care about the underlying value of the asset. They simply try to make a profit from small price movements. Traditional longer-term investors, however, take a stand on the value of an underlying asset, believing it to be either under- or overvalued. Traditional investors withdrawing from the market often cause price disruptions. During the 2010 flash crash many traditional investors stopped trading and thus added to the liquidity drain.

High frequency traders

The SEC report classified high frequency traders as market makers because of their daily frequency of trades without taking on significant net positions. High frequency traders were such a major group that the top 3 per cent of the intermediaries cited in the report included high frequency traders.

High frequency traders are major players in the SEC's report because they're first seen as providers of liquidity but then quickly they turn around to become takers of liquidity, thus contributing to the fast drop in prices.

Dark pools

Dark pools take their pricing from the lit markets. They're popular with banks, brokers and market makers who often route their orders first to a dark pool because of lower trading costs. The fees are much less than those charged by the exchanges.

As the lit markets began behaving strangely, spreads widened, liquidity disappeared and orders stopped being routed to dark pools because a proper price couldn't be made.

Tracking the 2010 Flash Crash, Moment by Moment

The following timetable looks at how the flash crash of 2010 happened so you can see for yourself at what time and in what order the events that caused the flash crash took place. These times are all based on the SEC's report. Remember, though, that many pundits disagree with the SEC's findings.

- **2:32 p.m.:** A large, institutional order, a mutual fund, entered the market and placed an incredibly large order of 75,000 contracts (valued at $4.1 billion), large even by E-Mini standards. During the past year only two other orders had been of a similar size, one of which was from the same institution. (Check out the nearby sidebar 'Identifying the suspected culprit of the 2010 flash crash' for more on this institution.)

Because the order was so large, the mutual fund used an algorithm, based on the order size on the overall volume of the previous minute, to enter the order bit by bit into the market. The algorithm was instructed to sell 9 per cent of the previous minute's volume, but no limit was placed on the number of contracts or a limit price. So whatever the volume was, the algorithm would continue to sell the equivalent of 9 per cent of the previous minute's volume.

Originally, the most likely buyers of these contracts were high frequency traders, but they tend to exit positions quickly. So while the mutual funds algorithm was trying to sell contracts in a market that was already under selling pressure, high frequency traders started to sell as well. This increased the selling volume. Because the mutual fund's algorithm was programmed to sell based on the previous minute's volume, it increased the amount of contracts it was selling.

- **2:41 p.m.:** Things came to a head as high frequency traders started to close their open positions by selling.

Although high frequency traders overall trade large volumes, they don't hold positions for a long period of time and their net positions at any given time are small. A whirlwind of volume hit the market, with HFT algorithms sending out a constant stream of orders mainly to sell, when in reality only a few players were left in the market, trading with a reduced number of market participants sending orders and trading, made up mainly of HFT algorithms. Not many market participants were left to trade and those that remained employed similar trading strategies, adding to the selling pressure.

- **2:45:13 p.m.:** Trading really sped up, with HFT programs desperately trading back and forth.

- **2:45:13 p.m. – 2:45:27 p.m.:** High frequency traders traded more than 27,000 contracts, which amounted to nearly half of the overall trading volume in the E-Mini. It took just 15 seconds for the E-Mini to drop 1.7 per cent. Between 2:41 p.m. and 2:45 p.m. the E-Mini had dropped a full 5 per cent, which was out-and-out panic.

- **2:45:28 p.m.:** A *stop-logic functionality* came into effect. Most exchanges have rules and regulations that try to stop crashes happening, and the Chicago Mercantile Exchange is no different. It stopped trading for five seconds to allow things to calm down and hopefully bring some buyers into the market to stop prices crashing further.

Buyers did start coming in after the pause in trading, and the market started to recover. Between 2:45 p.m. and 3:08 p.m. the market turned.

Identifying the suspected culprit for the 2010 flash crash

The SEC report clearly pointed the finger at the negative market sentiment at the time and the large, institutional sell order as being a trigger that sent the markets crashing. As is always the case with an inquiry, people wanted the guilty parties found. The SEC report was no different. Despite all the studies, from the report the SEC saw the cause as being the large order from an institutional investor to sell 75,000 E-Mini contracts. The SEC report doesn't mention the institutional investor by name, but reports have mentioned Kansas City-based firm Waddell & Reed as the firm that placed the contract order. Waddell & Reed has confirmed that it placed the order but has disputed that its order caused the crash.

A contributing factor to the market crash was that so many market participants simply stopped trading and withdrew from the markets. This took out liquidity from the market, meaning even a small order moved the price significantly. Although the volume of trading was high and may have given the appearance of liquidity, it was an illusion. For a market to be truly liquid, it requires many different types of investors with differing goals and investing time horizons. Because only a few players were left trading, they were all running similar trading programmes, trying to get in and out as fast as they could. This caused what the SEC report referred to as a *hot potato* effect.

A sudden disappearance of liquidity is always a contributing factor in a flash crash. A rapid loss of liquidity is difficult to see because trading volumes often spike up, yet there is no real accumulation of net positions one way or the other.

A way of spotting (though by no means completely reliable) is to have an algorithm that watches who is the broker or bank executing the trade. If there is a sudden disappearance of some brokers and only a few keep trading while overall volume goes up, it can be an indication that in fact there is a liquidity shortage.

✔ **3:08 p.m.:** The market had recovered to close to the same level as around 2:41 p.m., the beginning of the flash crash. During the period after the pause, the volumes traded were significantly higher than during the same periods in prior days' trading. This was caused by opportunistic traders trying to take advantage of the large volatility, including high frequency traders' algorithms continuing to trade. During this period of recovery the mutual fund algorithm kept selling contracts and the remainder of its order (40,000 contracts) was sold between 2:45 p.m. and 3:08 p.m.

The E-Mini is a contract that derives its value from the S&P 500, which in turn gets its value from the 500 stocks that make up the index. During this time, pandemonium was happening in the underlying stocks. As the E-Mini tanked, so did the S&P 500 index. During this panic, market makers and many market participants simply withdrew from the market, which caused a situation in which stocks were traded at ridiculous prices. If some unfortunate trader placed an at-market order to buy or sell and no one was in the market, his trade was executed at a *stub quote*, which is a quote placed by a market maker at a price far away from the normal price. For example, to buy at $0.01 or to sell at $10,000, these quotes are in the market so that a market maker can fulfil its requirement of offering both a bid and an offer. The New York Stock Exchange was forced to cancel some of these orders because they were clearly erroneous.

Criticising the SEC's Report

Not everyone accepted the SEC's report. Immediately upon release of the report, plenty of debate and criticism surrounded the accuracy of the SEC's findings.

One area of criticism is the SEC report's lack of accuracy. With traders going in and out of trades within milliseconds, the SEC's report is only accurate to the second. When there was a large amount of activity, probably very relevant activity, the SEC didn't even mention it.

The fact that it took more than five months for the SEC to come up with an analysis for trading that happened during one single day, the majority of the action in question happening within minutes of a day, is a sign that perhaps the SEC does not have the capabilities to properly analyse the modern market. Although it should be kept in mind that the time frames that required analysis were not long, analysing the amount of data that goes into those time frames was a massive task.

The SEC offers an official version of the crash, but it does fall short in being unable to explain in millisecond detail the events that happened during the crash. This has resulted in widespread scepticism as to its accuracy. Many have therefore turned to alternative sources to come up with a reason for the crash.

Considering an Alternative Version of the 2010 Crash

Plenty of alternative theories have surfaced to explain the causes of the flash crash of 2010, but one specifically attempts to explain it in minute detail backed up by data. The Chicago-based company Nanex LLC specialises in software that analyses market data. The company can analyse millions of trades per second. Its director, Eric Hunsader, is a vocal commentator on all things related to HFT. Nanex did its own study of the causes of the 2010 flash crash and came to a completely different conclusion than the SEC. You can find Nanex's final conclusions at www.nanex.net/FlashCrashFinal/ FlashCrashAnalysis_Theory.html.

Due to the detail and sheer amount of data, Nanex has been able to analyse that many market participants have accepted its alternative theory as a reliable analysis of the 2010 flash crash.

Nanex has been clear in disputing that the large, institutional order was the cause or effect of the flash crash. In its analysis, Nanex names Waddell & Reed directly. According to Nanex's analysis, the order placed by Waddell & Reed was an algorithmic order that was of a *low impact* variety, meaning that it shouldn't have driven the market down. Nanex's analysis is that the order 'never crossed the spread', which is a significant point. If this is the case, it means that at all times the institutional order was liquidity providing. The algorithm was in fact placing orders with a limit and waiting for someone to come and match them. It shouldn't have therefore been pushing down prices so aggressively.

In Nanex's opinion, high frequency traders who bought the institutional trader's orders and then turned around and aggressively sold, in 2,000 contract lots, what they had bought from (among others) the institutional trader caused the crash. *Aggressive selling* is equivalent to crossing the spread or taking liquidity, which means an order that takes out the bid and possibly the levels immediately following it depending on liquidity and the volume of the sell order. These types of traders, particularly in large volumes, move prices.

Because the E-Mini, the SPY exchange traded fund and the stocks that make up the S&P 500 are all connected to each other, any sudden move in one will affect the others.

The rapid, aggressive sale of 2,000 lot contracts in the E-Mini took out several levels of market depth. Nanex believes that this aggressive selling caused an 'explosion of quotes and trades in ETFs, equities, indexes, and options', with a delay of around 20 milliseconds, which Nanex points out as being the time it takes information to travel from Chicago (home of the Chicago Mercantile Exchange) to New York. This large amount of knock-on quotes overloaded the system, causing disruption in prices and the flash crash.

The following sections tell you about the two main alternative causes cited by Nanex as the reason for the flash crash. They look at the exact time that the crash began and what group they believe is at fault.

Finding the exact moment

Unlike the SEC report, Nanex dives down right into the milliseconds and has even given its opinion of the exact moment that the flash crash of 2010 started. As the Waddell & Reed order was being sold on the market, high frequency traders that had been on the other side of the order (buying) started to unload it (sell). According to Nanex, at 2:42:44.075 p.m. (notice that that's exactly down to the millisecond; pretty accurate, isn't it?) orders of 2,000 contracts started to hit the bid in an attempt to sell. More selling followed, which overloaded trading systems, and the linked markets couldn't keep up, causing pandemonium. Not until the five-second stop logic facility was triggered at 2:45:28 p.m. did the slide stop and allow buyers to enter the market and begin a recovery in prices.

Nanex's conclusion is simple enough to understand: 'In summary, the buyers of the Waddell & Reed E-Mini contracts, transformed a passive, low impact event, into a series of large, intense bursts of market impacting events which overloaded the system'.

Blaming HFT

Nanex's extensive study places the blame squarely at the door of high frequency traders, and unlike the SEC report absolves the large, institutional trader of all blame. Nanex's analysis states: 'HFT caused the flash crash.'

In Nanex's opinion, the act of high frequency traders reversing their position and beginning to sell aggressively, in effect taking liquidity from the market in sharp bursts, caused the crash. During this change, when liquidity was being withdrawn from the markets, related markets and stocks tried to readjust their prices, thus overloading the system and causing prices to go haywire.

As further proof that HFT caused the flash crash, Nanex published on its website an excerpt from a letter by R. T. Leuchtkafer sent just a few weeks prior to the crash in which Leuchtkafer describes exactly the same scenario that

Nanex had discovered in its analysis – one in which HFT is a liquidity provider, in essence a market maker, and then turns around and begins to suck liquidity from the market.

Analysing a Flash Crash

Flash crashes in single equities are a common event so you should be keeping your eye out for them. When you see such an occurrence, try to work out for yourself what happened and what caused it. You can then use that information in your own trading to help you avoid being caught up in a flash crash.

Take the following precautions in your analysis:

✔ **Actively follow the websites and blogs of prominent HFT commentators and experts.** You can find a good list to start with in Chapter 14.

✔ **Rely on social media.** Follow the commentators in Chapter 14 on Twitter, which is particularly popular with many HFT specialists. They often flag or comment on possible flash crashes and their causes.

✔ **Gather as much data as possible.** Data that is accurate by the second simply isn't good enough. You need to access charts and analysis that are accurate to the millisecond. Flash crashes are triggered within milliseconds. Flash crashes can also be finished in the same short amount of time. Often a small flash crash can point to a significant weakness in a particular stock or a market, and that's why you have to pay particular attention to anything that relates to a flash crash in a market or stock you trade in.

Part V
The Part of Tens

the
part of
tens

web extras

Get another helpful list of ten things you can do to get the best of your stock trade when trading through a dark pool at www.dummies.com/extras/darkpools.

In this part . . .

✔ Meet the many faces of the people and organisations that are moulding the modern high frequency and dark pool debate so you can always be up-to-date on any changes or events that may affect the world of dark pools and high frequency trading.

✔ Discover how to not get your investment profits eaten up by high frequency traders and to swim safely in the dark pools.

✔ Uncover what to discuss with your broker so that you get the best service possible.

✔ Know what to watch out for when you're about to make a trade so that you don't end up as fodder for the high frequency traders.

Chapter 14

Ten of the Best Dark Pool/HFT Websites

In This Chapter

▶ Following the most influential dark pool blogs

▶ Looking at both sides of the debate

▶ Keeping updated on changes in the dark pool universe

Dark pools and high frequency trading (HFT) have had a wild ride during the past decade. More recently, the debate about the pros and cons of dark pools has entered the mainstream. Because of the lack of transparency and the tendency by the media to oversimplify the subject of dark pools, a lot of wrong and misguided information is out there. As the conversation surrounding dark pools gathers pace, having reliable sources of information to turn to is important.

Dark pools are a divisive issue, so plenty of people are passionately opposed to them. You may have your own strong opinion or are still trying to figure out dark pools for yourself. Even if you do have a strong opinion, make sure that you follow the other side of the debate, because that side, with its influential people and their opinions, can affect legislators and public opinion also. Basically, knowledge is key.

In this chapter I look at information sources that can help you see both sides of the debate and keep you on the cutting edge of the dark pool and HFT universe.

Banker's Umbrella

The Banker's Umbrella (`www.bankersumbrella.com`) is my blog. It's one of the most popular blogs in the world on private banking and wealth management. The Banker's Umbrella touches on all subjects related to financial issues. Although it's not dedicated solely to dark pools, wealth management includes everything under the sun related to investing, so this blog also comments regularly on dark pools and HFT.

Banker's Umbrella is written in a conversational style assuming that you, the reader, have never heard of the subject of any of the articles before. It doesn't assume any prior knowledge on the reader's part. Because of its easy-to-read, educational format it's a great place to discover dark pools. The website is written in a relaxed style, it pulls no punches, is informative and is always humorous.

The Banker's Umbrella is also very active on social media, so if you have a question you can go on Twitter and send a tweet to @BankersUmbrella and often you'll get a quick reply. Who knows, perhaps you'll even inspire a blog post. How's that for service?

Don't be fooled by the easygoing conversational style, though. The Banker's Umbrella is influential. Articles that have appeared in the blog have been published in full in mainstream media like the *International Business Times*, and the analysis from the Banker's Umbrella has been cited in the *Financial Times*; even the US House Committee on Financial Services follows what is written there.

Haim Bodek

Haim Bodek is a former quantitative analyst (commonly referred to as a *quant*) who wanted to be a heavy metal rock star. (You can read more about quants in Chapter 7.) Although the rock star thing hasn't happened yet – perhaps because he doesn't have the hair for the job – plenty is still going on in that bald dome of his. Bodek was for several years a builder of trading programmes and algorithms for banks and hedge funds. He also ran his own trading company called Trading Machines.

Bodek began writing critical articles on HFT and in effect became a whistle blower on the industry. His articles revealing collusion between exchanges and HFT firms resulted in his book *The Problem of HFT — Collected Writings on High Frequency Trading & Stock Market Structure Reform* (CreateSpace Independent Publishing Platform). Bodek's extensive experience working at the very centre of the modern market makes him a voice to listen to.

He's currently head of Decimus Capital Markets with a self-professed goal to 'level the playing field' against the adverse effects of HFT. You can follow him at www.haimbodek.com and also on Twitter: @HaimBodek.

Themis Trading

Themis Trading (www.themistrading.com), founded by Sal Arnuk and Joseph Saluzzi, is an institutional brokerage firm that is critical of the HFT arena. Sal and Joe run one of only a handful of active blogs concentrating on dark pools and market structure that is actually entertaining and not too academic. If it's happening in dark pools or HFT, you can be sure Themis will have an opinion.

Arnuk and Saluzzi authored a book, *Broken Markets: How High Frequency Trading and Predatory Practices on Wall Street Are Destroying Investor Confidence* (Financial Times/Prentice Hall), describing how in their view HFT is detrimental to investor confidence. US senator Ted Kauffman wrote the foreword, which tells you that legislators are paying very close attention to what they're saying. Both Arnuk and Saluzzi can be found on Twitter: @ThemisSal and @JoeSaluzzi. They are also regular TV pundits on the subject of dark pools and HFT.

Scott Patterson

Scott Patterson is a journalist for the *Wall Street Journal* and could well be described as the definitive author on dark pools and HFT. He has authored two books: *The Quants: How a New Breed of Math Whizzes Conquered Wall Street and Nearly Destroyed It* (Crown Business) and *Dark Pools: The Rise of the Machine and the Rigging of the US Stock Market* (Crown Business).

Patterson tells a great story, and his books read more like a detective novel than a theoretical dissection of market structures. Both his books are a great way to meet the types of characters that operate in the dark pool and quant universe, instead of just describing the strategies used (oh, he does that too). You really get a feel of the personal struggles and intrigue that are involved in this world of electronic trading. You discover all about the personalities of the players, which gives a true human element to his writing. He can convey complex issues in a non-technical way, making the writing entertaining and educational. Patterson is also active on Twitter: @PattersonScott.

Zero Hedge

Perhaps the most famous blog on markets in general is Zero Hedge (www. zerohedge.com), a site with a cult following. Zero Hedge dwarfs all other financial market blogs. Started in 2009, the blog is written in an activist style and is highly critical of markets. It has managed to remain shrouded in mystery. It's still not entirely clear who started it and it's believed to be edited by several people.

Many of the articles are published anonymously, often signed with the name Tyler Durden, the character from the book and film *Fight Club*. Zero Hedge defends the use of anonymity, saying that it protects the impartiality and integrity of the articles. This has certainly worked, with about 200,000 followers (Yes! Two hundred thousand!) on Twitter. Many people love it and many people hate it, and it's certainly worth following. It's updated several times a day; you'll never be short of opinion if you follow Zero Hedge.

CFA Institute

The Chartered Financial Analyst (CFA) is a professional credential for financial analysts. (Clue is in the name, isn't it?) It's a rigorous programme that requires the delegates to take three exams over the course of several years. After you're accredited with the CFA, you definitely know your way around a company balance sheet and stock exchange press releases. It's an internationally recognised programme and is often a prerequisite for analyst jobs within the financial industry.

Now you don't need to devote several years of your life to getting a CFA after your name, but the institute itself you should be following. In addition to running the CFA programme it publishes regular papers and organises events all over the world on issues affecting the securities industry.

The CFA Institute is interested in ethics, legislation and best practice, and it is very much an industry thought leader. Since the financial meltdown of 2008 the CFA has increased its attention on ethics within the industry. Because dark pools have faced so much criticism, due to their lack of transparency, it's a subject that the CFA Institute follows closely.

You can find the CFA Institute at www.cfainstitute.org, and you can also follow it on Twitter: @CFAInstitute. You won't find the CFA very engaging on social media; its Twitter feed is predominantly a stream of advertisements for its content. But if you skim through the self-advertising tweets, you'll often find up-to-date, important information regarding the comings and goings of the financial sector.

Nanex

Like most people, I have no idea what Nanex really does. According to its website (www.nanex.net), it has some kind of Telefeed from something to somewhere run by its own computer program. If you can work out what on earth it is Nanex does then let me know, but one thing is clear: Nanex knows the electronic trading world inside out.

It's the Nanex research that's interesting. If you look at its website, it looks a little crude and confusing, but Nanex has been able to blow open some very interesting information regarding what is happening in electronic trading.

Nanex made big news when it released its research 'The Great Fed Robbery' in which it claimed that data from the Fed had been leaked early to certain traders so that they could profit from an upcoming press release from the Federal Reserve. Remember, this is HFT, so when Nanex claimed early, it meant milliseconds early.

The report made Nanex instant news headlines, and legislators and journalists stood up and took interest. Several HFT trading firms disputed Nanex's findings and Nanex has become very much a love or hate firm in the debate regarding HFT.

Eric Hunsader heads Nanex and is an active tweeter (@Nanexllc). You won't be surprised that he doesn't pull any punches and is very critical of the HFT space. Like him or loathe him, you ignore him at your own peril, because what Hunsader says people listen to and discuss.

You'll really want to take a look at the charts and graphs Nanex produces. They're highly detailed visual depictions of market activity broken down into millisecond increments. They'll give you a real understanding of how orders move in HFT trading. The sheer speed and volume that is involved when there's a big news event is amazing. It can be a little disconcerting too because when you see the graphs and look at the time it takes for the action to happen you'll notice that the market reaction is over within milliseconds. A bit too fast to react to if you are sitting by the trading screen eating a doughnut and drinking coffee.

Able Alpha

Able Alpha, which was formed in 2007, is a firm that provides computerised trading services. Basically, that means it builds algorithms. Check out its website at `www.ablealpha.com`.

The founder, Irene Aldridge, is a staunch defender of HFT. She is the author of *High-Frequency Trading: A Practical Guide to Algorithmic Strategies and Trading Systems* (John Wiley & Sons, Inc.), which explains in detail how algorithms are built and used. The book is in its second edition and is required reading for some university courses. Aldridge has a background in financial engineering and has worked on Wall Street and taught quantitative finance in universities.

Aldridge's style is academic, so it helps if you've versed yourself well on algorithms and computerised trading before diving into her material; otherwise it can be a bit heavy going.

You can find her on Twitter: @IreneAldridge. She isn't the most engaging of tweeters, mainly commenting and linking to articles she finds interesting. It's good to keep in mind that she is very much a market commentator, so her social media presence isn't focused solely on HFT but rather markets in general.

The Trading Mesh

Formerly known as the HFT Review, the Trading Mesh (the former site htfreview.com now redirects to `www.tradingmesh.com`) is a social network and website for the electronic trading industry. On the site you'll find blogs, expert interviews and white papers all related to the world of electronic trading. Mike O'Hara, a former financial technology consultant, and Ken Yeadon, a former HFT trader and venture capitalist, founded the site.

If you register as a user then you'll be able to customise your own dashboard by choosing what experts and blogs you want to follow. You can also manage your own newsfeed and even post your own blog posts.

The site is run based on advertising revenue, so some of the content, for example white papers, is only accessible by paying for it.

A vast amount of material is available on the Trading Mesh, often written by industry insiders in industry jargon, so if you're new to electronic trading then it might be a bit sleep inducing. After you master all the jargon (from this book, for instance), it does make for educational stuff. Many quants come here to hang out and show their peacock feathers, so you get a great insight into the electronic trading industry.

The expert interviews on the site are of particular interest because they're up-to-date opinions from those in the industry who matter. Interviews are also more conversational in tone and make for easier reading than detailed technical articles on the intricacies of a certain trading programme.

Healthy Markets

The goal of Healthy Markets (www.healthymarkets.org) is to improve trust and transparency within the financial markets. You can find opinions on the debate around market structure, which dark pools and HFT are very much part of.

The site itself is new. The reason to follow it closely is that one of the people behind Healthy Markets is Dave Lauer. Lauer is an active commentator on all matters relating to HFT, dark pools and overall market structure. He's a former quantitative analyst and high frequency trader, and he has been involved with building and designing trading programmes. Lauer has appeared before Congress as an expert, and his opinions have regularly been quoted in the financial press. His style of discussion is unique among those involved in the HFT debate in that his is a voice of reason without the emotional fervour that seems all too common for HFT pundits. He is active on Twitter: @DLauer.

Chapter 15

Ten Ways to Swim Safely in Dark Pools

In This Chapter

▶ Looking out for high frequency strategies

▶ Following the trading book

▶ Gaining market intelligence

*T*he more insight you have into how dark pools and high frequency trading (HFT) affect the securities that you're trading and what your broker is doing with dark pools, the higher your chances for getting a better price for your trade. This chapter gives you ten easy tips to help you to protect yourself when planning on placing a trade.

Watching the Bid Offer Spread Action

When you decide to make a trade in a specific stock, keep an eye on the spread – not just for a few minutes before you place your order, but well in advance. Pay close attention to the bid offer spread for days and even weeks in advance. Know what the average spread is and whether any situations occur when it's wider or narrower than the average.

The *bid offer spread* is where the trading is done. The *bid* is the price that someone is willing to pay you to buy your stock, and the *offer* is the price at which someone is willing to sell you his stock. Check out Chapter 3 for more in-depth information about bids and offers.

To get accustomed to following a bid offer spread, look at a slow-moving stock that has bids and offers coming up on the screen at a pace that the human eye can follow. Mid to small cap stocks can be good for doing this. With very *liquid* stocks (stocks that have a large number of investors placing orders both on the buy and the sell side of the order book at various prices) prices move at a frantic pace.

Watch how the bid offer spread moves and get a feel for it. When you see a bid appear at the top of the trading book, watch to see whether there is any change in the other side on the offer. Is it removed? Is there a change in the amount of shares on offer? Also watch the best bid. If you've placed an order at the best bid and there's a wide spread, does a new bid come in front of yours at a slightly higher price immediately after you've placed yours? If this does happen then it's an indication that there's a trading algorithm running. Remove your order and see if the bid changes again to confirm that there is an algorithm in the market. In such situations you can discuss the bid with your broker and ask him to route the trade through a dark pool instead of the lit market.

Checking to See Whether Your Market Order Slips

If you look at the bid offer spread and you place an at-market order to buy, check to see whether your order gets executed at a different price from the offer at which you placed the order. This kind of situation can happen in fast-moving markets. Nothing illegal is happening, but it may indicate that HFT is going on and you're the prey.

If your order gets executed at a higher price than when you entered your order, particularly when the stock is trading steadily with no market impacting news, this situation may be an indication of offers being removed when firm purchase orders are made. This concept is termed *phantom liquidity* – when you think there's an order there, but it isn't real. Phantom liquidity is one reason to avoid at-market orders, even if the security is offered at a price that you're willing to pay. Use a limit order instead of an at-market order. You may lose the trade, but at least you won't be executed at a completely different price to what you were expecting.

One sign that a predatory high frequency algorithm is operating is that as soon as your order has been executed (at a price some distance from what you expected) the bid and offer slide back to where they were just before you placed your order.

Identifying Changes in the Bid Spread

When using a limit order, look out for changes in the spread that may indicate algorithmic trading. In this situation changes occur most obviously when you place an order either at the top of the bid or offer. Check to see whether another order for a slightly better price overtakes you.

Remove your order immediately by choosing the cancel order in your broker-age account or by calling your broker, and see what happens. If the order that popped up in front of you suddenly disappears, it's always good to play a bit of cat and mouse and try it again. Do the following to see whether the same thing happens:

✔ Place your order.

✔ Another order comes up in front of yours.

✔ Remove your order.

✔ The order that was in front of yours disappears.

If you see this happening then most likely an algorithmic program is at work.

Watch the order book, and if or when the price hits your intended target, place a limit order at that price. The downside to this strategy is it can be quite time consuming, because you need to spend time watching the order book closely and then inputting the trade manually. You should also ask your broker whether the order can be executed in a dark pool with your limit price. Check out Chapter 8 for more on this strategy when placing a limit order.

Spotting 100 or 200 Block Orders in the Order Book

Although the overall amount of securities traded on markets has grown, the actual size of individual trades has decreased. Due to the rise in HFT, the average size of a settled trade is nowadays around 100 to 200 shares. If you regularly see orders in the trading book popping up in lots of 100 or 200 shares then more than likely they're automated trades. Detecting the volume at a particular price can be difficult because they're often bundled together.

Have a look at the additions or deductions coming into the volume numbers on the order book, such as an offer of 800 shares changing to 1,000 shares. Changes like this in one stock don't tell you anything, but if you look at both sides of the trading book and see these changes in vol-umes of 100 and 200 share lots, it's an indication of the presence of HFT algorithms in the market.

Checking for Your Limit Number in the Order Book

Before you place a limit order in the market, have a look at the order book and the price level at which you're placing an order. Make a note of the number of shares in the book at that level. When you place your order, immediately look to see whether your order pops up on the order book. In a very fast moving market in a big name stock, doing so may be impossible because orders are coming in all the time – particularly the closer you get to the best bid and the best offer.

If your order doesn't come up on the screen, your broker is probably trying to trade it through a dark pool. If you have access to the exchange's own trade confirmations through your broker or you have direct market access and your broker's sign doesn't show up with the same price and volume as your order, it's a sure sign that your trades are done through a dark pool. The best way to confirm is to ask your broker.

Verifying the Stock's Spread

First you should check the *spread* of your stock (the difference between the bid and the offer prices), and then calculate the average price, which is also known as the *mid-price*. The mid-price is important because your broker might automatically route your order to a dark pool first or you may want to request your broker to send the order to a dark pool. Dark pool orders tend to be matched at the mid-price. The only way you'll know if there is another order on the other side in a dark pool is by sending the order into the dark pool.

By using the mid-price you get the possibility for a better price than what is available at the displayed market. This is particularly important with illiquid stocks where the spread can be significant.

If your broker is using a dark pool, even if you sent an order as an at-market order and there is a matching order in the dark pool, you should be executed at that better price (the mid-price). However, there's always the temptation and the possibility of front running, when someone trades against you by executing the trade at the mid-price ahead of you and then trading with you against the best bid or offer.

These front running antics are difficult to prove, but there have been reports that these happen. By using a limit order at the mid-price, you have the possibility of getting a better price than what is visible on the order book.

Recognising Flash Crashes

If a stock has had a flash crash, beware. Basically, *flash crashes* are a sudden drop in the stock price over the period of a few milliseconds up to a few minutes. Flash crashes in a stock are indicative that high frequency traders may be active in that stock and liquidity can disappear quickly. You're susceptible to getting your order filled at a poor price if a flash crash happens. Your biggest risk of getting your order executed at an inferior price is if you're using stop loss orders, because a stop loss order will turn into an at-market order when the limit is hit. In a flash crash, liquidity disappears and the price at which the stock is then executed can be a significant way off the stop level.

Check the history of the stock, starting with a normal chart to see whether it has had any crashes in price. Make sure that the chart has a *high and low marking*, which is the highest and the lowest price. Candlestick and bar charts are good examples. Flash crashes happen within a trading day and can be over in minutes or even seconds. If you don't have a high or low price on the chart, flash crashes simply won't show up on the chart.

Even the use of historical charts isn't reliable because in the case of a flash crash it's possible that trades are *broken*, meaning that they're cancelled afterwards as invalid. Depending on how the historical data is gathered and reported, it's always possible that the full scale of the crash won't show on the chart.

Use Google Finance and Yahoo Finance to check for any news reports citing a flash crash in the stock during the last year. Flash crashes in individual stocks can be common, and they aren't necessarily big news, but they're often mentioned in corporate specific news.

With individual stocks that have a history of flash crashes, you may want to avoid trading in them altogether. In such cases you'll most likely be trading only against high frequency traders. If you don't have access to algorithmic trading tools, you'll be at a distinct disadvantage with your trades being filled at inferior prices.

Reading a Tick-by-Tick Chart

Charts are a great way for you to visualise how the market moves and protect yourself when investing in dark pools. The tinier the increments you can use, the better the chart is. By using tick charts you can see how active algorithmic trading is when it comes to a specific stock, because tick charts show bursts of orders better than traditional charts based on time. You can obtain most charts in tick-by-tick increments showing the amount of transactions rather than time. You choose the increments you want to use. For example a 100-tick chart will show the last 100 transactions including their high, low, open and closing prices.

By checking the tick data you can spot what kind of situations algorithmic traders use to trade in the stock. This should give you valuable information on how to place your own trades for better execution.

Talking to Your Broker

In order to protect yourself when investing in dark pools, discuss with your broker in detail how he routes and executes trades.

Knowing how orders are routed and who your counterparts are is extremely important and can make the difference between consistently getting a bad price or a fair price. Make sure that you're aware of all the steps in the order executing process.

Questions you should be asking include the following:

- ✔ Do you receive payment for order flow?
- ✔ Do you use dark pools to execute client trades?
- ✔ What dark pools do you use?
- ✔ Do you use special order types?
- ✔ Do you modify client orders into special order types?
- ✔ Can I instruct on how I want a trade routed?

You need to have the ability to control as much of your trade as you can, should you feel the need to. Transparency between the broker and you regarding order execution is an important trust issue. Don't be afraid to ask for answers to these questions in writing. You can verify that your orders are being executed the way you want. If a situation arises in which regulators move against your broker, or a dark pool used by your broker, having written confirmation of how your trades should have been executed gives you the option to demand reimbursement.

Sometimes a broker doesn't know exactly how a trade is routed. If so, don't be afraid to be demand clarification. If your broker doesn't understand your questions, ask to discuss the questions with his superior.

Perusing the Executed Orders

Exchanges publish executed trade data, sometimes at a cost. Make sure that you read these executed orders. This information gives you the time stamp, price, volume and brokers involved on each side of the trade. With this information you can see who the main players are in the stock, which brokers are most active and which are not.

To better visualise all this information, I suggest putting the data into Excel and then creating a chart.

Do some research into the main brokers to see whether they're known for using algorithmic programs. This information isn't always something they want to advertise, so look to see whether they offer services that may be used by high frequency traders, such as co-location and direct market access.

Sometimes you see traders pop up on the screen who are continuously selling stocks at certain increments, which can alert you to iceberg orders and hidden volume.

Also look for orders reported into the book that are of a larger volume than the average order. These are often block trades that the broker has been working on over some time. After the order is filled, the broker then reports the trade to the exchange. In all likelihood these trades were executed in a dark pool and show a major dark pool player within that stock.

Chapter 16

Ten Common Algorithmic Strategies

*T*rading strategies are meant to make a trader money and to control risk at the same time. In this chapter I share some of the most common automated trading strategies used today. Many of these strategies aren't new; they're simply tried-and-tested ones that have been speeded up by computers and fast data feeds. For those trying to trade manually without the help of a computer algorithm, the old strategies have become redundant because no human can keep up or react manually to the speed of an algorithm.

Automated trading strategies fall into two categories. First you have those that are used by institutions and large investors to place orders that have minimal price impact on the stock or index they're trying to buy or sell. Then you have the strategies used by high frequency traders and market makers to trade in and out of stocks quickly. In this chapter I cover both categories.

Market Making

Market making is the process of providing simultaneously a bid and an offer on a trading exchange. A *bid* is a quote to buy and an *offer* is a quote to sell a security. Market making aims to make a profit from the price difference between the bid and the offer. Many high frequency trading (HFT) strategies are derived from market-making-based strategies because these HFT algorithms involve constantly placing limit orders in the market.

Two types of market making exist:

- ✔ Market making as purely a trading strategy without any obligations to post a bid or an offer

- ✔ Being a *designated* market maker, which comes with an obligation to quote a bid and offer. With this obligation (and added risk) comes some advantages such as paying lower transaction costs on the market and even getting rebates (see the following section).

Algorithmic trading is well suited for market making because traders can quickly adjust quotes by price and size based on a computer program. Modern market making done with algorithms also involves the use of special order types, which you can read more about in Chapter 9. The market maker uses special order types to get the best possible position in the order book queue.

Getting Liquidity Rebates

Certain exchanges and dark pools pay traders to post orders on their trading book. This is known as *providing liquidity*. The more liquidity there is in a stock, the more interesting the dark pool or stock exchange is to investors because they become more confident that even their largest orders will be filled, due to the liquidity available.

A stock exchange or dark pool makes money by charging a fee for all executed trades. When it pays for traders to provide liquidity it splits this fee with the trader who's agreed to provide liquidity. In effect the liquidity provider acts as a market maker (see the preceding section).

A trader operating a liquidity-providing program posts bids and offers to the order book. Each time a market order or a matching-limit order enters the dark pool or exchange, the trader earns a rebate from the exchange. This form of trading doesn't require selling a stock at a higher price than buying it. A trader can buy and sell a stock at the same price or even at a small loss; provided that that loss is offset by the rebate, the trade still makes the liquidity-rebate trader a profit.

Some exchanges pay rebates to take liquidity. *Taking liquidity* means buying limit orders that are in the order book with a market order or a matching-limit order.

With a liquidity-rebate strategy an algorithm places limit orders in the order book and after an order is executed the algorithm immediately places another limit order to liquidate that position. For example, if a trader has a rebate agreement with an exchange, the algorithm places a limit-buy order and after that's executed the trader earns a rebate. The trader now simply needs to sell that same position at a price that, including the rebate, leaves the trader with a profit. An algorithm posts limit orders simultaneously at bids and offers, and as orders are matched and earn a rebate the algorithm sends an offsetting order so that the open position is liquidated and the trader earns another rebate.

If the trader has a liquidity-taking agreement with another exchange, she can immediately make an offsetting at market order in the other exchange to earn a rebate. This way she doesn't have to take the risk of posting a limit order at an exchange in the hope that it will be executed.

Deviating from the Norm with Statistical Arbitrage

Statistical arbitrage, often referred to as *stat arb*, makes use of short-term price differences in the same security traded on different venues or of short-term price differences in related securities. The idea behind statistical arbitrage is that price discrepancies in securities markets exist but they quickly disappear. Algorithmic trading is particularly suited to statistical arbitrage because the time period for which a price difference exists may be just a fraction of a second.

For example, when trading the same security in different venues an algorithm follows all the venues, lit and dark, that the security is traded in. Whenever a price discrepancy occurs, that algorithm buys in the market with the lower price and sells in the market with the higher price, thus creating a profit. The window of opportunity for such discrepancies is short, normally just a fraction of a second; therefore this type of trading is best suited to algorithmic trading.

In the case of trading in related securities, statistical arbitrage becomes more complicated. *Related securities* can be an index and a single stock inside that index, or it can be a single stock and other stocks in the same sector. A statistical arbitrage strategy in related securities involves collecting lots of historical data and determining the normal relationship between the two related markets. Whenever a deviation from this norm occurs, the algorithm makes a purchase or sale.

For example, if an algorithm is designed to follow a basket of medical stocks the prices of which tend to be closely correlated, whenever algorithm detects a statistical difference between these stocks, the algorithm sells those that are overpriced and buys those that are underpriced. The basis of this kind of trading is that a normal balance and correlation exists between these related stocks and that any differences in the norm eventually revert back to the norm.

Catching the Short-term Momentum

Much of the trading done by large institutions is designed to have a minimum impact on the price of the stock they're trading. Strategies based on *momentum* attempt to discover and profit from short-term trends. A trend is generated when a change in the volume of a stock being traded occurs and that change in volume moves the stock's price. Unlike strategies that try to capture the bid-offer spread, a trend lasts for some time and moves several price points. Trends can be caused by

- ✔ News flow regarding a stock or the market in general
- ✔ Large orders that are discovered by other traders, who then start to trade in the direction of the large order, causing a price movement

A short-term momentum strategy isn't concerned with finding the bottom or the top of the trend. The main goal is to see when the trend is forming and get out of the trade before the trend changes again. This means that a short-term momentum strategy tries to catch the middle part of the trend.

Employing Latency Arbitrage

Modern equity markets are complex: they handle large amounts of data and require highly technological systems. This complexity means that inevitably data is processed at different speeds. *Latency arbitrage* makes use of the differences in speed between market participants. Latency arbitrage tries to makes use of the superior speed of high frequency traders, using among other things high-speed fibre optics, superior bandwidth, co-located servers and direct-price feeds from exchanges to make trades ahead of other market participants.

The theory behind latency arbitrage is that in the US the consolidated feed that determines the National Best Bid and Offer (NBBO) of all the US stock exchanges is slower than what high frequency traders are able to receive via direct data feeds from stock exchanges. With the superior speed the algorithm of a HFT program is able to read trade data faster than many other market participants by seeing prices a fraction of a second ahead of the Securities Information Processor (SIP) feed, which is the consolidated US stock exchange price feed. This, in essence, gives the HFT program information before it hits the official market (the SIP feed) and allows high frequency traders to see where prices are moving before other market participants.

Following the News

All trading is about information and using that information to make investment decisions. *Information-driven strategies* refers specifically to the use of news data by algorithmic-trading programs to make trading decisions.

Algorithms are programmed to read and analyse news reports by major news agencies and even social media. Any kind of news releases that may affect market prices triggers a buy or a sell from the algorithm.

The use of information-driven strategies by high frequency traders has become so popular that some news services package their news releases in a way that makes it easy for algorithms to analyse them. For example, they use set terms to describe a positive or negative event so that an algorithm can act based on key words in the news release. News services also place news reports on servers located in key geographical locations (such as important financial centres) prior to their scheduled release. This cuts down the time it takes for information to travel from one place to another. News service providers charge extra for these types of services.

The use of social media is increasing for information-driven strategies, as is evident in the hacking of the Associated Press Twitter feed. In 2013 a hacker tweeted that a bomb had been set off in the White House and the president had been injured, and this resulted in an immediate drop in the equity markets globally as algorithms analysed this 'negative' news from a reliable source and began selling in the market.

Igniting Momentum

If an order you send into the market could instigate a price movement and you know that it could do so, you have a chance to trade profitably. This is what *momentum-ignition* trading strategies attempt to do. The goal is to trigger other algorithms and traders to begin trading in a stock and thereby create a price movement. In essence, what a momentum ignition strategy does is try to trick other market participants into thinking a significant price movement is about to happen so that they begin to trade. In this way the price move becomes a self-fulfilling prophecy: traders think a price movement will happen, and their actions create a price movement.

A momentum-ignition strategy involves sending out large amounts of orders into the order book and then cancelling. This gives the appearance of a large change in volume in the stock and can trigger orders from other traders, thereby beginning a short-term price trend. The momentum ignition strategy involves executing the actual intended trading position before trying to ignite the price movement. This means that first a trade is executed that doesn't move the market significantly. This allows the trader following the momentum-ignition strategy to get into the price movement before it's triggered. After the trade is executed, the momentum ignition is set by sending a flurry of orders and cancelling them in the hope that other traders will follow and thus move the price. Then, as the price begins to move, the trader employing the momentum-ignition strategy exits her original position at a profit.

Momentum-ignition strategies make use of special order types (see Chapter 9) and traders can execute them only with algorithms that can send out and cancel large amounts of orders in a short timeframe.

Combining a Dark Pool and Lit Markets

Dark pools take their prices from the displayed markets. The most common way to determine a price in a dark pool is to take the average price of the bid and the offer on the displayed markets; this is known as the *mid-price*. A combined dark-pool and lit-market strategy takes a position in either a dark pool or a lit market and then attempts to move the mid-price by posting a bid or offer in the lit markets and then executing the trade for a profit in a dark pool. This is a form of gaming the price (for more on gaming, see Chapter 11).

For example, a high frequency program has an order to buy at the best bid. When that order is executed, the algorithm immediately places another bid in the lit markets one price point away from the best offer. This moves the mid-price up. Then the algorithm places a sell order in a dark pool with the hope that it will be executed at the mid-price, which will be a higher price than the algorithm bought the stock at. After the sell order is executed in the dark pool, the bid in the displayed market is cancelled and the process begins again.

This requires speeds in the milliseconds and is only possible with an algorithm. The order placed in the lit markets that moves the mid-price and the order entered into the dark pool happen nearly simultaneously, and the cancellation of the order in the lit markets happens almost instantaneously after the order in the dark pool is executed. If the cancellation of the order in the lit market isn't done, there's the risk that the order will be executed and resulting in a new open position and a losing trade.

Factoring in the Participation Rate

Large institutions employ *participation-rate strategies*, which involve using an algorithm to execute an order with the intention of the order having a minimal price impact. The algorithm is programmed based on past information regarding the volume of the stock traded. The algorithm looks at the average volumes based on the time of day traded or the volume traded in a prior period during the same day; for example, the last minute. It then places an order as a percentage of volume for the period it's using as a comparison; for example, 2 per cent of the volume in the previous period.

Participation-rate strategies were the very first types of algorithmic strategies and they're the most basic and simple to execute. Other market participants with algorithmic trading strategies can discover the most basic of participation-rate strategies. That means participation-rate strategies can be risky to implement because a significant risk exists of moving the price against your order. This is why more complex participation-rate strategies have been designed, aimed at fooling other traders. In these more advanced participation-rate algorithms the participation rate isn't constant; a random participation band exists – for example, 2 to 8 per cent of the previous period. This makes it harder for other market participants to discover a large order.

Weighting for Time

Large investors use *time-weighted strategies* to try to minimise the price impact of a large order. As the name implies, this strategy uses time to split a larger order into smaller chunks that are then entered into the market over a specified period of time. If, for example, a fund manager wants to sell an order of 9,000 shares, she could use a time-weighted algorithm over the period of two hours, so the algorithm sends an order of 750 shares to sell to the market every ten minutes.

Commonly, a time-weighted approach mixes up the number and the time it sends the orders into the market, so every order isn't exactly the same size or at exactly the same interval. This is to disguise the order from predatory traders trying to find a larger order in the book and trade against it.

Chapter 17

Ten Things to Know About Market Microstructure

As markets have got faster, you'd think that trading has got easier: that hurdles and complexities disappear as trade execution becomes quicker and quicker. In fact, the opposite has been the case. As markets have gained speed and technology has advanced, the business of making a stock transaction has become more complex.

Market microstructure is concerned with how trades are executed in the markets. Speed isn't the only consideration, although it's important. Market microstructure is also concerned with how data is transferred from one place to another, what route it takes, what computer languages it uses, and the tools and infrastructure required to move the data about.

High frequency trading (HFT) has played a major role in the forming of modern market microstructure. The goal of HFT is to be first in line in the order book whenever a high frequency trader wants to make a trade. Technological advances have been driven by the demand for speed and fast execution by high frequency traders.

When execution happens in microseconds, as it does today, what happens becomes ever more important. Because of the super-fast speeds you can't see it with your eyes, but you can be knowledgeable as to what's happening. When you know the basics of market structure, you can prepare yourself for any changes that legislation or technological advances bring to the market and adjust your trading accordingly.

In this chapter I outline ten important aspects related to market microstructure, giving you the necessary knowledge of the complexities of the modern trading market.

Market Access Speed

Stock exchanges and dark pools are businesses; therefore they're about making money. Their business is built around executing trades: they charge a fee whenever there's a trade executed, and this is how they make their money. To get more trades executed, exchanges and dark pools need more trading volume. So they're constantly trying to get trading volume. Stock exchanges and dark pools compete with their peers and are in a constant battle to offer better execution to their clients. Better execution comes down to speed and being first in line in the order-book queue.

With such a large part of overall trading volume now coming from HFT, dark pools and stock exchanges need high frequency traders to increase their volumes and trade executions. To get more HFT volume, exchanges and dark pools sell access to their own markets at different levels. They offer market participants different types of services with a choice of speed of access to the stock market or dark pool in question. The more speed required by a trader, the more the trader has to pay the exchanges and dark pools.

Thanks to modern technology the speed offered by the stock exchanges and dark pools is fast by any measure. The slowest levels of service are calculated in the milliseconds and the fastest in just microseconds.

The needs of high frequency traders pose a problem for the exchanges because of the risk and the perception that some participants (the high frequency traders) are able to gain an advantage over other market participants. The justification given for this tiered system by the exchanges and dark pools is that the services are open to all, provided they can pay for them.

The different levels of access on offer create a market where participants are trading at a different speeds. If your trading strategy is based on pure queue position and speed then you need the best speed of access to the markets, otherwise your trading strategy won't work, regardless of how good it is in theory.

Order Types

Order types play an important role in market microstructure. Orders have become more and more complex: they're now routed to multiple venues while traders attempt to get the best possible queue position when they place their orders. Queue position is key as the better the placing in the order queue the more likely it is that the trade you want to make is executed.

In the competition for queue position orders now contain more information than just the price and volume of a trade. They can remain hidden, showing only a part of the full order, or they can change position and price in the order book automatically based on the type of order sent. The different types of orders available in all the markets combined, displayed and dark pools, number in the hundreds.

Displayed stock exchanges and dark pools have their own specific special order types that define how the order interacts with the rest of the order book. To be able to trade effectively and profitably and get the best possible execution for his trade, a trader needs to know the specifics of the order used. Because orders include many different variables, choosing the right order manually is rarely a good option. Most of the new types of orders are designed with algorithmic trading in mind and they're built into the trading algorithms so that the algorithm makes the decision on the best order to choose for a particular trade.

Networks

How fast data is transmitted from one place to another is right at the heart of market microstructure. There are several different types of technologies used to improve the speed of data transfer as market participants, particularly high frequency traders, try to get an edge over their competitors with the speed at which they conduct their trading. This demand for ever-faster speeds has resulted in a race to be as fast as possible; the goal is to get as close to possible to the speed of light. Here are three ways to transmit data:

- **Fibre-optic cables:** High frequency traders use fibre-optic cables to receive and send out data in microseconds. These cables offer reliability and bandwidth that can transport vast amounts of data at high speeds. Large investments are laying out fibre-optic cables to connect financial centres in different geographical locations.

- **Microwaves:** Microwaves (the actual waves, not the ovens!) are used to send data via microwave towers. Using microwave technology is a faster way to send data than using fibre-optic cables, but the downside is that weather conditions can affect the speed and also fibre-optic cables can still carry more data than microwaves.

- **Laser beams:** The latest technology; originally used by the military to send information. Laser technology offers better bandwidth than microwaves and isn't as susceptible to weather conditions. As the race for the fastest possible speed continues, the use of laser technology is likely to increase.

Algorithms

Trading manually has become harder and harder. Trade execution has accelerated to speeds that are counted in microseconds, and the proliferation of market venues has brought about an ever-increasing need for algorithms to do what humans aren't fast enough to do.

Traders need algorithms to make all the major decision that go into making a trade decision today. They use algorithms to decide when to execute a trade, at what price, at how large a volume and in what venues. When other market participants are able to execute trades in just a few microseconds, a trader must have access to algorithms that can compete, or at least level the playing field, with the fastest participants.

High frequency traders and institutional investors use algorithms to handle the complexities of the modern market. An algorithm can quickly make a decision as to the best possible price to make a trade and it can also run trading strategies that take on market risk by taking positions in a stock in the attempt to trade profitably. (For more on algorithmic trading strategies, see Chapter 16.)

An important part of algorithmic trading is that it takes out the human emotional aspect of trading. Trading decisions made by algorithms are based solely on the data analysed and not the whims, fear and greed of an individual human trader.

Fragmentation

Fragmentation in the markets is on the increase. This means that you can now trade the same stock on multiple venues simultaneously, in both displayed stock markets and dark pools. In the US alone you have more than a dozen displayed stock exchanges to choose from, in addition to all the dark pools.

Having such a large choice of different trading venues to choose from adds to the complexity of the market. No longer does a trader send an order to a stock exchange and wait for the trade to be executed; now the trader has to decide to which venue to send his order and why.

All the different venues have their own levels of access and their own specific order types, and at any given time the prices on offer in the various venues differ, as does the amount of orders and available volume on the exchange or dark pool. This makes the simple process of sending an order to the market a difficult proposition for a trader. To be effective and to obtain the best possible execution requires an understanding of the specifics of each possible venue and also the ability to quickly choose the best venue. With so many variables at play, the only way to handle such complexities is to use a computer algorithm that makes those decisions when the trade is sent.

Order Routing

Order routing means the way an order travels through the different market venues, both the dark pools and the displayed stock markets. The control over routing order depends on the access you have to the different market venues and the services provided by your broker(s) and the exchanges and dark pools you trade in.

Order routing is a computerised affair in which smart order routers are often used. Smart routers are programmed so that they can send out orders based on the output of a trading algorithm, choosing the best venue for a particular order. They can split the order up and send it to multiple venues, executing in both dark pools and displayed stock markets. Prices change constantly within milliseconds and *liquidity* (the availability of a stock in a specific venue) differs from venue to venue. That's why the ability to split orders up and route them to multiple venues is crucial.

Regulation

The modern markets are a result of regulation. In addition to their own internal rules all markets have rules created by national regulators and must operate within the regulatory framework. Regulation is concerned with providing a fair and efficient market for all market participants. It's the foundation of how a market operates, and exchanges and pools have to adhere to certain ways of executing a trade.

Because of the rapid advances in technology the market is constantly evolving, and regulators are trying to keep up with the changes and adapt legislation to fit the modern market. This is a difficult task because legislation moves at a slower pace than the advance of technology.

Concerns about the fairness of the market for all market participants have increased scrutiny by regulators, and a drive exists for new legislation to handle the changes in the market. Changes in legislation mean changes in the market and how orders are executed and displayed.

You need to closely follow the legislative discussions and suggestions made by market participants and legislators, because they will, when implemented, have an effect on how trades are executed and as a result they'll also have an affect on trading strategies, making some strategies obsolete and bringing about new strategies. If you're not aware of how market regulation affects the markets you trade in, your trading results will suffer. Flick to Chapter 6 for the lowdown on regulation.

Transparency

Because of the fragmentation of markets and, particularly, the emergence of dark pools, transparency has become a concern. *Transparency* refers to the way information is available to various market participants. The more transparent the market, the larger the number of market participants who receive the same information at the same time. The less transparent the market, the smaller the number of participants who have access to the same market information. Transparency is often an issue of trade-flow data, getting information on orders coming into the market regarding the price and volume of a stock.

A market that's lacking in transparency creates opportunities for those traders who have priority access to information that other market participants don't have. The increase in the amount of dark pools has resulted in a decrease of transparency. Only certain people see the incoming trades before other market participants, which creates opportunities for those trading with superior information.

Regulators are concerned with providing a market that's both transparent and efficient. But they have to consider the fact that large, institutional investors require a certain level of anonymity and lack of transparency in the execution of their trades, so that they can execute large orders with minimal price impact.

How much information is available to market participants and in what time-frame affects the fairness of the overall market.

Price Formation

Often people think that the price of a stock is based purely on supply and demand. However, nowadays market microstructure also plays a part. For example, the prices on US stock exchanges are consolidated into one price, the National Best Bid and Offer (NBBO). Then the best prices to buy and to sell are always first line (known as *protected*) regardless of which displayed market they're quoted on. Once the best price is executed, other orders in the order books of the various exchanges can be traded. This can have an effect on the overall price of a trade that's larger than the volume on offer in the NBBO.

Dark pools take their prices from the displayed markets, so the level of the spread of the best bid and offer in the displayed markets (and, in the US, the NBBO) can determine the price of the execution on a dark pool. Knowing these rules gives the opportunity for traders with the speed and the necessary algorithms to manipulate the price in the dark pools and trade profitably by combining their trading between the displayed markets and dark pools (more on this in Chapter 16).

Displayed stock exchanges and dark pools each have varying ways of determining a price. Some match trades throughout the trading as orders come in and others run an auction at set times. Knowing the process of price formation in the various venues where you're trading allows you to make the best decision on when and where to trade at any given time.

Market Intermediaries

Placing an order into the market can and often does involve several intermediaries. When you send your trade orders through a broker, he often uses his discretion as to how he executes your order. This may require the use of other intermediaries in the effort to execute your order. The broker may have control of the routing of the order and he may split the order into several parts, executing those parts in different venues. Your broker may try to execute the order internally against one of his own client's orders. Your orders may go through a dark pool before going to an exchange, or the broker may package the order and sell it to traders who pay your broker so they can execute their order against yours. This practice is known as *payment for order flow*.

The goal of the intermediary should be to provide you, the trader, with the best possible execution of your trade. But the incentives that your broker has may not always be aligned with yours. Therefore knowing all the possible intermediaries that your trade may go through while it's being executed is important. Then you know your trade is executed in the best possible way, a way that satisfies you.

Index

About the Author

Jay Vaananen is a former senior private banker, having worked in Luxembourg advising high net worth individuals on their investments. Jay has more than a decade of experience working in a multi asset-environment. He has advised, invested and traded in bonds, equities, derivatives, funds, ETFs, structured products, hedge funds and commodities. If it was available to trade on the financial markets, Jay has dealt with it.

Jay is also the founder of The Banker's Umbrella (`www.bankersumbrella.com`), which is the world's most popular blog on private banking. The Banker's Umbrella is a humorous yet informative blog on all things that relate to the financial world. The Banker's Umbrella is widely read and has often been cited by news media, including the *Financial Times*. Jay is a source of advice and opinion among leading financial commentators, often giving his unique and no-nonsense opinion on wealth management and current financial news. His articles have been widely published, including in the *International Business Times* and *eFinancialCareers*.

Jay has also been a visiting lecturer at universities, discussing and teaching about the global financial markets. Jay spent his childhood in the UK and was educated in Finland where he graduated with a degree in finance and risk management. He currently writes full time and splits his time between Luxembourg and Finland.

Dedication

To Pipsa for putting up with me. To my sister Eeva and her husband Chris for always believing in me and encouraging me. To Harlan, Carmen and Zeny: without you this wouldn't have been possible. Finally and most importantly, to my children Ella and Ensio. Daddy did this so he could be home more. It worked.

Author Acknowledgments

It's no exaggeration to say that this book has been a huge challenge. How to put into an understandable format as much as possible about a very secretive and non-public area of finance that affects everyone who operates within the financial world? I owe a debt of gratitude to all my peers in banking whom I have had the honour to work alongside and meet along the way. Special thanks go to Markus Lindahl, without whom I would never really have set off on this journey. To Ilpo Aarnikoivu, Jyrki Lehtinen, Juha Pukkala and Veli-Matti Jaatinen whom I sat with on the same desk for so many years, and to Kaj Backstrom and J-P Virtanen with whom the time was shorter. The discussions, debates and arguments with you gentlemen have always left me with a greater understanding of what it was we were involved with.

Lastly, everyone at John Wiley & Sons, Inc. To Claire Ruston for getting this started. To Chad Sievers and Martin Key for their superb editing that vastly improved this book. Finally and especially to Michelle Hacker and Annie Knight for their saintly patience and steadfast professionalism. We got there in the end.

Publisher's Acknowledgments

Project Manager: Michelle Hacker

Project Editor: Simon Bell

Acquisitions Editor: Annie Knight

Development Editor: Chad Sievers

Copy Editor: Martin Key

Proofreader: Charlie White

Technical Editor: Russell Rhoads, CFA

Project Coordinator: Melissa Cossell

Cover Image: © iStock.com/BlackJack3D

Take Dummies with you everywhere you go!

Whether you're excited about e-books, want more from the web, must have your mobile apps, or swept up in social media, Dummies makes everything easier.

Visit Us

Like Us

Follow Us

Watch Us

Join Us

Pin Us

Circle Us

Shop Us

FOR DUMMIES

A Wiley Brand

BUSINESS

978-1-118-73077-5

978-1-118-44349-1

978-1-119-97527-4

MUSIC

978-1-119-94276-4

978-0-470-97799-6

978-0-470-49644-2

DIGITAL PHOTOGRAPHY

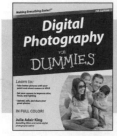
978-1-118-09203-3

978-0-470-76878-5

978-1-118-00472-2

Algebra I For Dummies
978-0-470-55964-2

Anatomy & Physiology For Dummies, 2nd Edition
978-0-470-92326-9

Asperger's Syndrome For Dummies
978-0-470-66087-4

Basic Maths For Dummies
978-1-119-97452-9

Body Language For Dummies, 2nd Edition
978-1-119-95351-7

Bookkeeping For Dummies, 3rd Edition
978-1-118-34689-1

British Sign Language For Dummies
978-0-470-69477-0

Cricket for Dummies, 2nd Edition
978-1-118-48032-8

Currency Trading For Dummies, 2nd Edition
978-1-118-01851-4

Cycling For Dummies
978-1-118-36435-2

Diabetes For Dummies, 3rd Edition
978-0-470-97711-8

eBay For Dummies, 3rd Edition
978-1-119-94122-4

Electronics For Dummies All-in-One For Dummies
978-1-118-58973-1

English Grammar For Dummies
978-0-470-05752-0

French For Dummies, 2nd Edition
978-1-118-00464-7

Guitar For Dummies, 3rd Edition
978-1-118-11554-1

IBS For Dummies
978-0-470-51737-6

Keeping Chickens For Dummies
978-1-119-99417-6

Knitting For Dummies, 3rd Edition
978-1-118-66151-2